Finding Davy Crockett

Family Stories and Genealogy

Mark Standley, PhD

Connie Fluegel, MA

Compiled by Mark Standley, PhD and Connie Fluegel, MA using
ChatGPT, written stories from Mark's Grandfather, James Patterson
Crockett III ('Jimmy Highpockets) the autobiography of David
Crockett, and other print and human resources.

Printed in the United States.
First edition, March, 2024
Book Cover Design: Luis M. Ramirez
www.luisramirezweb.com
ISBN (paperback):979-8-9888093-3-3
HC V. 2.5

Other Books by Mark Standley

- Digital Storytelling: iMovie (2010), PowerPoint (2010) (Visions)
- Technology Standards (2008) (Visions)
- Global Project-based Learning (2010) (Visions)
- Our Museum of Us: Curating Your Family's Stuff into a Digital Future (2020)
- Teaching Jesus: What & How Jesus Taught. How We Teach Jesus (2023)

Book of Questions:

- Teaching Powerful Storytelling (2012)
- Unmanned Aerial Systems for Schools (2016)
- Drone Essential Knowledge and Skills (DEKS) (2019)
- Fishing on Kayaks (2021)
- Touring on Bikes (with David Plaskett) (2020)
- Learning to Become an Old Man with Dr Jim Giles and Dr. Scott Hoyer (2021)

at amazon,com

Table of Contents

Quotable Crocketts

Winning Shooting Matches

David Crockett (age ~18)
"I was going to hunt for deer, as they were pretty plenty about in those parts; but, instead of hunting them, I went straight on to the shooting-match, where I joined in with a partner, and we put in several shots for the beef. I was mighty lucky, and when the match was over I had won the whole beef. This was on a Saturday, and my success had put me in the finest humour in the world." (Chapter III, page 136)

James P. Crockett III (aka Jimmy Highpockets) (age ~16)
"The whole community would gather with their guns and form a line across the prairie. They would walk abreast of each other in line and cover the ground for miles around. There would be people from the surrounding towns, Merchants, Bankers, and others that came for the sport. There would be an assortment of guns. Some of the men from the towns would have expensive guns. A cash prize was given to the one who killed the greatest number of rabbits. Highpockets had never been permitted to go on a rabbit drive because it was a rule that everyone must have a gun, so now that he had a gun he felt qualified to go and when the line formed he fell in at the end of it, right by a big banker who had a shiney high powered gun. The people began to laugh and point at Highpockets with his little rifle, walking along beside the big banker with his expensive gun. The banker looked down at Highpockets with a sneer and asked him what he thought he could kill with that "Pea Shooter." But as they marched on side by side, the rabbits began to jump up here and there. Highpockets could see a puff of smoke shoot out of each gun until the rabbit would quit running and start rolling. It was a rule that the man nearest the rabbit should have the first shot. If he missed then the next man down the line shot, and so on until the rabbit was killed. When the rabbit ran out away from the line it was easy to hit, but if it ran parallel with the line the man on the end of

4

the line would usually be the first to get a shot at it because the others did not have room to shoot without shooting too close to the other men down the line. Highpockets was on the left end of the line and when a rabbit came his way he had a clear field and plenty of time to draw a bead, so he seldom missed his rabbit and to the dismay of all those whole poked fun at his "Pea Shooter" and the constarnation of the big banker with his high priced gun, Highpockets came in with the most rabbits killed on the drive. He received $25.00 in prize money and a considerable amount for the rabbit ears. He did not get very much recognition for having accomplished this feat as the other members of the hunt seemed to resent such an insignificant person taking the prize money. But he was accustomed to being snubbed so he did not expect any-thing else. He laughed to himself as he hid his money in an empty horse medicine can on a rafter in the top of the loft. He felt that it would be safe there as he was the one that always had to climb up in the loft to throw down hay. This was the beginning of High-pockets' savings account which saved the ranch in the years to come." (Chapter II, page 23)

How This Book is Organized

This book is a collection of stories by two adventuresome Crocketts - David Crockett (August 17, 1786 - March 6, 1836) and James Patterson Crockett III (March 3, 1897- October 26, 1967) (aka Jimmy Highpockets). David's brother, James Patterson (March 7, 1784 - 1834) was James Patterson Crockett III's second great grandfather. David was James P. Crockett III's second great grand uncle. Both collections of these stories are autobiographical and written 127 years apart in 1834 and 1961 respectively recounting their lives and adventures.

The first section shares the stories of Jimmy Highpockets - the nick name and pen name for James P. Crockett III. His autobiography (1961) tells his experiences in third person narrative growing up as the child of a poor sharecropper in West Texas. He tells about his beloved animals, homespun humility, closeness to nature, beloved rifle, being looked down upon because his poverty and few clothes (his nickname 'Jimmy Highpockets' due to pants too short as he grew), entrepreneurial spirit, marksmanship prowess, romance, and ultimate overcoming obstacles in the environment and society. James P. Crockett III went on to soldier in World War I, had two families, and a successful business career. He left us his families and the Jimmy Highpocket's stories as part of his legacy.

David's autobiography (1834) presented in full here recounts in first person narrative his youth, poverty, hunting, marksmanship prowess, romance, families, beloved rifle, closeness to nature, soldering, homespun humor, innovations in politicking, legislature experiences, overcoming obstacles both real and in society, and ultimately his departure from Tennessee. He preferred being called 'David' although the popular sentiment at the time, through Disney's character on TV, and folks even today refer to him as 'Davy.' In this book we will refer to him as he wished. David left us two families and his autobiography as part of his life's legacy. He went on to Texas and the Alamo and became the legend, 'Davy

Crockett,' he was then and is today.

The middle section of this book explores the world of genealogical tools and societies today. Using ChatGPT we use this computer knowledge to bring a fresh look at the myriad of tools individuals, families, and professional genealogy researchers can use. We describe the difference between officially accepted research findings (i.e. accepted applications for Daughters or Sons of the American Revolution, which we hold up as a gold standard) and the mishmash of computer generated legacies we call "barking up the wrong family tree." The online tools have never been more prolific and never more susceptible to fiction. Using these tools in concert with genealogical societies nationwide and certified genealogical professionals requires certain "proofs" - typically certificates of birth, marriage and death to ascertain truthful lineage. Other records such as church, property ownership, wills, military, letters and journals are invaluable. This section shares those tools, links, a sampling of societies, "do's and don'ts" and where to get started.

Read this book as a collection of two stories written by family (David and James P.) who have values, experiences and virtues in common. These narratives and the genealogy tools in this book led us to enjoy, laugh, cry, and befriend our ancestors, David Crockett and James P. Crockett III, as if we all were sitting around a campfire with rifles, hunting dogs, chewing tobacco, and stories of hunting 'varmints' and an intense love of the woods in our backyards. You'll have to bring your own coonskin cap to read this book and sit alongside us and these storied storytellers.. This book brings to life how family stories and genealogy bring our dearly departed ancestors and their lives into our own.

We have also shared a list of books, magazines, and links that we found helpful in our research. Also you'll find a glossary of common terns used in genealogy and historic societies to further your knowledge and understanding when using these tools.

Introduction (Mark)

We are in the GreenHouse Cafe with plates topped by the broken bits of consumed sandwiches, half empty glasses of ice tea, and our various manilla folders with notes and family records tucked neatly within. Front and center on the table sits my Sons of the American Revolution (SAR) application. It sits like a shiny tabloid unearthed from years of unknown and unlisted ancestors whose DNA I carry forward into my generation of baby boomers. Sitting next to me is Bill Soles, President of the local SAR chapter and Wanda Pooley (a SAR genealogical research extraordinaire and member of local DAR) who are reviewing this tabloid before sending it and my application fee to Washington, DC to be reviewed for accuracy and acceptability. The question lingering over the table is 'Did he get it right?'

Across the table is Connie Fluegel, taking notes from our conversation for our book you are reading now. With Wanda's remarkable research skills, Connie was inducted as a member of the Daughters of the American Revolution (DAR). Connie too has a family member who served in the American Revolution. Her sense of pride and humility is evident as she breathes in this new truth in her family's history - they (on her father's side) too are all related to a 'patriot.' Their patriot was a drummer in New York. A drummer wiling to stand in front of the armed soldiers behind and before him and drum up the enthusiasm and marching instructions for his revolutionary brothers in arms against the British soldiers and Loyalists. Connie's patriot was their family's brave agent of change, when how that change was to turn out was not certain. A family value for Connie and relatives to bring forth into our current times.

And the same question hovers in my mind of our family's first discovered patriot, Edward Boone. More to research but we found he was not only related to Daniel Boone, famous frontiersman, but also related to John Crockett and Rebecca Hawkins, mother and father to David Crockett and his eight siblings, one of who was James Patterson Crockett, 4th great grandfather to my baby boomer siblings and myself. If our research turns to be correct, we not only get the decided honor of joining many other members of the SAR, whose patriots are well documented because of the verification process, but we also net a famous American in one of the branches of our family tree - David Crockett - about as famous a person in America and Texas as there is. But this is not the first time we learned we might be related to this celebrated frontiersman.

We first learned of our possible connection from our mother's (Julia Crockett) aunt (Dollie Mabel Crockett Rogers) when living in a farmhouse on the prairie in Kansas. On a visit to Aunt Dollie in Kansas City the question came up - "Are we somehow related to the Davy Crockett?" "Sure we are!" she exclaimed, "We've known it all our lives." Well , that's quite a notion to put into the mind of a ten year old boy, who enjoyed his .22 rifle, rabbit and raccoon hunting in the creek bed next to his family farm. "Davy Crockett!" My imagination soared! Only years later did I realize that hearing it from Aunt Dollie made it exciting, but not necessarily true. The truth came from the stories of our mother's father (James Patterson Crockett III) and actual research in the genealogical tools described in the mid section of this book.

Grandfather's stories of his time growing up in West Texas gave us the narrative path and curiosity to look further. He wrote stories using his nickname and pen name, Jimmy Highpockets. He sent them from Huntsville, Texas, where he and grandmother raised our mother and three siblings, to us as children as we moved around the country finally landing back in Texas near our families. More on Grandfather and Jimmy Highpockets stories in the first section of this book. To us a children and later as adults, Grandfather's stories carried us like a covered wagon back into our family's past. We had to explore and find out more.

That exploration took the form of one of our siblings carefully copying and sending a binder of the stories to each of us. We could then share them reading to our own children. Another sibling began using the new genealogy tools to probe further back into the Crockett family tree. She came up with a very plausible connection to John Crockett and Rebecca Hawkins and their nine children. She and Connie teamed up to dig further. We then recruited an expert in Wanda, to do the detailed research and documentation. Within a few days of her deep dive, Wanda came back to us with a big smile. "Yes, you are a relative of David Crockett, and yes you have a Patriot." It brought Aunt Dollie's claim of connection from a young boy's coonskin cap dream to a marble monument proven because of the careful research through the documents.

And that proof sat on our lunch table among the plates, glasses, and manilla folders with Wanda, Connie, Bill and myself. A shiney tabloid of research and proof born of family lore, grandfather's stories, our collective curiosity and cooperation, and true genealogical research in the form of an application to become a member of SAR, one of America's most respected historical societies. The impact of the moment was like someone turning on the lights in a room that heretofore we had been stumbling through with a mere flashlight; a moment of shear clarity from the years of curiosity and stories to knowing through genealogical documentation and proof.

Connie and my path through our family's past and genealogy is not unique. Many families want to learn of their ancestors and their lives, whether early to America or later in our history as landed immigrants with their concomitant stories. Many families rely on the hearsay of family stories or the computer generated lineages and go "..barking up the wrong family tree." In this book we'll provide detailed tools for searching for the documentation and verification through researchers and historical societies like DAR and SAR to be sure you are accurate. We'll also share Grandfather's Jimmy Highpocket's stories, as well as the autobiography of David Crockett so you get in the tree with them and their 'varmints' in their lives. We hope you'll see as we have the wonderful spirits and values these two adventuresome Crocketts shared in lives separated by over a century. In this book we want to show how stories and genealogy research can lead to the most remarkable revelations about family.

And one step further...

David Crockett was a most remarkable man. Our Grandfather, James P. Crockett III was no David Crockett, but in his own way was remarkable as a father, grandfather to our family, and writer of his early life. They both had remarkable childhoods. Their stories are here in this book for you to enjoy and absorb. Dr Don Frasier, a world-class historian who heads the Texas Center at Schreiner University in Kerrville Texas, once made an insightful point describing the early life of George Washington. Dr. Frasier opined that there was nothing extra ordinary in Washington's early life. Dr. Frasier believes that most famous people hit an 'inflection point(s)' in their lives that shifts them into history as the remarkable people we remember today.

Dr. Frasier's insight is significant for this book. David Crockett did not start out remarkable. As you read through his life story in his own words; you begin to see the 'inflection points' that propelled him from backwoods childhood to legislator and hero of the Alamo. In a much smaller context you'll read James P. Crockett III's inflection points that led him from dirt poor son of a sharecropper in West Texas to launch his life as family and businessman. In this book we invite you to read and recognize the inflection points in this two adventuresome Crocketts' lives so you can begin to research the lives and inflection points of your own family's ancestors. We believe in this way we can begin to see and recognize, even move, the inflection points in our own lives and those of our children.

Family stories and genealogy are about choices in lives. We make choices that move us forward and choices that move us back from ourselves, our goals, and our family values. Learning from the choices our ancestors had and made can teach us volumes about the way we recognize and make choices in our own lives. These insights can also help guide the choices our children have and make. Genealogy is about accurately knowing our family, the choices they had and made to better recognize why some are more famous; other infamous.

We believe our legacies are to accurately, factually represent and celebrate our ancestors' past, to give light to shared values and quality choices, and to guide our family, society, and future generations.

Introduction to Jimmy Highpocket's Stories (Mark)

Isn't life strange! We grow up surrounded by family and stories but fail to recognize the beauty and depth in the narratives until long after we lose these dear relatives who lived remarkable lives in their own time and in their own way. Such was the case for our maternal grandfather, James Patterson Crockett III (pen name: Jimmy Highpockets).

In this book we have collected his stories as a young boy/man growing up in West Texas the very poor son of a sharecropper and very rich in life experiences. From his adult home in Huntsville, Texas he would type letters and stories to his daughter, Julia Crockett Standley (Mark's Mother). Mom would readm(five siblings) these letters and stories to us as we moved about the country away from Texas and away from our grandparents in East Texas who were always eager for our Christmas visits.

The affect of those holiday visits was always warm, loving, and caring. The stories and laughter flowed as we enjoyed our grandparents' attention and divinity candy, aunts and uncles' playfulness, and the adventure-filled back yard full of cats, swing sets, and chinaberry trees. Those visits bring back so many happy reflections growing up, but lost in our memories are the details of Grandpa's and Grandma's stories. So, it is a tremendous stroke of luck and love that Grandpa persisted to record these stories of his youth. Sent to us in letters over time and to the different places we lived, the stories became serialized which gave us time to absorb them. They anchored in Grandpa's life and values growing up poor and resilient.   Mom would have us draw and color pictures from the images in the stories which she sent back to Grandpa much to his delight. It was clear in his letters accompanying the stories that he was as delighted to share them as we were to hear them. The stories became a thread that drew us back to Grandpa, East Texas, and the values that held our family and individuals together.

Fast forward to my 9 year-old self living with our family on a farm near Holton, Kansas. Our farm and surrounding country side held a bonanza of rabbits, raccoons, frogs, coyotes, and birds. My siblings and I would explore the creeks, ponds and woods very much like our Grandpa recounts in his Jimmy Highpocket's stories. We did not have to imagine the 'yelps' of the 'wolves' (probably coyotes) in his stories as we watched them range across the cut alfalfa fields next to our farm house in fall and winter. We hunted raccoons for pelts to sell and rabbits for the subsistence meat for our family dinner table just as Jimmy Highpockets did at our age. We were living his stories except without the poverty of his sharecropper world and family.

For a moment let's return to the fall, 1964. Mark was living in northern Kansas. Our family took a trip to Kansas City to visit Grandpa's sister, Dolly (Dolly Mabel Crockett Rogers). Among the hugs we came to meet another of Mom's relatives - Aunt Dolly Crockett. There was that name and unanswered question again that trailed behind us like something big - 'are we related to Davy Crockett?' When we got the courage to ask Aunt Dolly, she shrugged it off like we were asking if the sky is blue.
        'Of course!' Davy's one of our great grand uncles."
I was frozen in time and disbelief. Was that remotely possible? How would we know? Who else could we ask to find out more? More questions than answers until now.

We returned to the hunting hollows and sandy creek bottom trees for our hunting and adventures. We wore our coonskin caps with more reverence and pride with the possible connection to

"Davy.". And as in most things with young children, the bright lights of our potential famous relative faded. We moved on to a new pony, the lively times at our two-room school house and the Wizard of Oz on our black and white TV. Still, seeds planted just right in a child's mind can mature into big dreams.

Some fifty years later those dreams re-emerged in our sisters who carefully collected Grandpa's letters and Jimmy Highpockets stories into three ring binders and sent them to the rest of the siblings. What a treasure trove to receive as an adult and share with our own children. Then one curiosity led to another and our older sister began internet and Ancestry searches into the Crockett lineage. As she searched and began to verify, it began a process that led to this book. We wanted to answer the questions about family stories, hearsay, and how do families research and verify the truthfulness of claims to famous and infamous people.

More on this in the section, "Finding Your Ancestors". For now, let's go back to Grandpa and his stories that put us on this path. Let us allow Grandpa to introduce himself as Jimmy Highpockets from one of the letters that accompanied the stories. Here is James Patterson Crockett III (aka Grandpa) introducing us to Jimmy Highpockets - himself, his nickname and eventually his pen name in his own written words:

****

"This little boy was living on a farm away out on the prairie. He had a dog and he built a house for it with his tools. He was always catching squirrels, rabbits, and O'possums, and he built cages for them with his little tools.

He had lots of friends among the animals on the farm. He would get up early in the morning. His first job would be to carry feed to the Hogs. When the Hogs heard him coming they would get up out of their straw beds, and start begging for something to eat. The old mama hog would say Whoue-Wah-Wah, and the little pigs would say Whee-ee-ee. The old papa Hog would Whoff-Whoff-Whau. When he got the Hogs fed, then he would go feed the cows. The cows would say Moo-Moo. The old papa cow would say Muea-Meeau. He would have to go out into the pasture and hunt the little calves. They were kept in the lot all day and turned out in the pasture at night.

He would have a lot of fun going after the calves. Sometimes it would be dark, and he would be afraid of the wolves, and snakes, but his faithful pal "Old Spot" who was half Greyhound and half Bulldog, would always be by his side, so he would feel safe. If anything showed up that looked like it might hurt the little boy, Old Spot grabbed it by the back of the neck, and shook the life out of it.

This little boy had lots of friends out on the prairie too. As the Sun came up, and Crows, and the Hawks, and the birds started hollering at each other, and chasing each other. The Crows would chase the Hawks, and the Scissortail birds would chase the Crows. The dew on the Spider Webs, which the Spiders wove on the Broomweeds, would look like diamonds in the Sun. Drops would form at each place where the web crossed. The Spider would catch him a fly for breakfast. The Horned Toad would get up on top of an Ant Hill, and make his breakfast out of the Ants as they came out of their home on the ground. All the birds and animals were eating their breakfasts. By the time this little boy and "Old Spot" rounded up the calves and got back to the barn, he was so hungry that he rushed to the house and ate a big breakfast himself. He ate so much that he got so fat that his clothes were too small. His pants were so short that his friends called him HIGH POCKETS. This was the Nick Name for the little boy all his life.

Hope you enjoyed the story, and will be looking forward to the time you can come see the old timer again."

Lots of Love,
Grandady

JIMMY HIGHPOCKETS

CHAPTER I

Highpockets was born on a tenant farm in west Texas. He was
the seventh child in a family of twelve. His father was honest
and hard working but had too big a family for his income. He
started out as a sharecropper, and all he was ever able to produce
in abundance was a family. Highpockets got his nickname from
other boys poking fun at him because he was always outgrowing
his pants; and not being able to get new ones. He would have to
wear them until they were so tight the bottoms would be above
his knees. Highpockets developed an inferiority complex because
he was always pushed aside by his older brothers and was forced
by them to do any unpleasant task that had to be performed. One
of the most unpleasant jobs was to climb up a ladder through a
scuttle hole in the big barn loft, before daylight every morning,
and throw loose hay down for the livestock. This barn loft was
a roosting place for screech owls, wild barn cats, skunks, and
snakes. These varments would den up in the tons of loose hay
and every time Highpockets would start up the ladder the cats
and owls would make a dive for the scuttle hole which was their
only way of escape, trying to get out before he got up in the loft.
He was in constant fear of being scratched and bitten or sticking
his pitchfork into a skunk, which was worse. Another very unpleasant task was to bog through filthy hog pens and take out
new born baby pigs so they could be fed on a bottle until they
were strong enough to stand on their own feet and get out of the
way of the old sow when she went to lay down. When one of the
livestock was injured and worms got into the wound he was the
one who would have to forget his fears of being bitten or kicked,
and dig out the filthy worms.

He had to go out in the big pasture before daylight in the morning
to drive up the workstock. He would whistle in the dark to keep
from hearing the varments slithering through the tall grass. One
morning about daylight he was walking down a cow trail and he

walked right up on a diamond back rattle snake, coiled up ready to strike. He was walking so fast he could not stop in time so he jumped as high as he could, thinking he could jump completely over it before it could strike. As he went over, the snake struck and its fangs caught in the heady sole of Highpocket's brogans. He hit the ground stomping his feet and was able to crush the snake's head with his heel before it could bite him. The thing he dreaded most on these early morning roundups was wolves. They were so thick people even had to keep their dogs house in at night, as wolf packs would make their rounds every night and any living thing that was not house in or well guarded would be devours. Horses out on the range would always graze in groups with the colts protected and when the cattle bedded down at night they would always do so with the little calves nestled near their mothers heads. If an animal died or became injured so that it could not protect itself or get away the wolves would gather from all directions and devour it completely. This gathering would create a melee that could be heard for miles around. The wolves would yip, howl, and snarl and fight until the last bit of flesh was eaten from the bones. In their savage fighting they would slash each other and at the sight of blood would rush in and completely devour the injured wolf. By the time the animal was cleaned up there would be a patch of ground that would be completely bare of grass, which would be covered with the bones of the dead animal and the wolves. One morning Highpockets started out on the early morning roundup.

The big pasture was south of the farm house, and a blue norther was howling across the prairie, which blew the sound away from Highpockets and kept him from hearing the dine of the wolf pack. In order to be able to locate the herd in the dark, a bell would be strapped on the neck of the old lead mare. Highpockets could not hear the bell above the howling of the wind that morning, but he figured from past experience that he would find the herd on the south side of a hill. The big pasture sloped gradually for about a mile to a creek. The south bank of this creek was about twenty feet high. It was sand rock formation and at intervals along the bank there were ravines cut in it where cow trails led through, up the hill on the other side of the creek. After hunting his way up the creek in the dark Highpockets came to a familiar opening in the sand rock and climbed up and came out on top of the hill. He plodded on for a short distance down the south slope of the hill when he found a little colt all alone. He felt sure his miserable hunt in the cold was over as this- so he thought would be where the herd was bedded down- but when he got far enough down the hill that it broke the bowling of the blue norther, he was horrified by the yipping and snarling of a wolf pack in the valley just below him. He was so badly frightened that his only thought was to get away from there quick, so back up the trail he went. In his scramble up the trail he frightened the colt and it also made for the opening in the sand rock. In his excitement Highpockets stumbled in the dark and fell down the hill to the bed of the creek. He was knocked unconscious by the fall and his left leg was broken. When he awoke he was laying on the soft dry sand of the creek bed and the colt was nuzzling his nose. After the colt got over its fright it had started back to locate its mother, and when it got to where Highpockets was laying in the creek bed it stayed there. It was several hours before Highpockets' family found him and carried him and the colt to the house. Horses are able to sense the approaching of a storm or a blue norther, before there are any signs visible to the human being. When a herd of horses are warned by this horse sense that a storm is coming, they put on a performance that resembles an Indian War Dance. They curl their tails over their backs, their heels up in the air and run around and around. The earth cracks open on the prairie when it gets real dry, and sometimes the cracks get wide enough that animals step in them and fall. While taking part in the pre-storm horse festival that was being performed before the blue norther hit, the Mother of the colt stepped in a crack in the earth and fell and broke her neck. The wolves discovered her first and were so busy devouring her that they had not found the helpless colt when Highpockets made his appearance. Since Highpockets' father was only a share-cropper and did not own the mother of the colt he told Highpockets they would have to take it back to the rancher. When they took it back to the rancher he told them that he did not have time to bother with raising it on a bottle, and that if Highpockets wanted it he could have it. As Highpockets was not able to feed it his family objected to him keeping it as they did not want the trouble of taking care of it until he got well. The rancher had a little girl about the age of Highpockets who agreed to take care of it until Highpockets got well. This little girl's name was Grace. Grace kept the colt at the ranch until Highpockets got well and then he brought it home. He had to help milk the cows every morning and every evening, so he got an empty medicine bottle and rubber nipple, and when he went to milk he would fill the bottle up with warm milk and give it to the colt. He fed it this way until it was old enough to eat grain and hay. His family laughed at him and called the colt his baby. But after it began to grow up into a beautiful animal the whole family became attached to it and they named it Babe. Highpockets and Babe were constant companions When Babe was one year old she began to shed her dull smudgy looking colt hair. Her new coat of hair was the color of red gold. It sparkled in the sun light and rippled as her skin flexed over the muscles of her legs and shoulders. Her mane was real black and soft, and it grew so long that it could be parted in the middle and tied together under her neck. She had a long black wavy tail. Her hoofs were black but legs were white about half way up to her knees, and she had a white star right between her eyes.

CHAPTER II

High Pockets had a hard life. He had to work hard from about four o'clock in the morning until after dark at night. There was never any time to rest. He had to chop wood, pump water for the house and milk the cows and feed all the livestock. He would come in so tired at night that he could hardly wait to get his clothes off before he hit the hay. When time came to get up in the morning he would be so sore and stiff he could hardly move. He would have to put on the same clothes he wore the day before, as he only had enough for a change once each week. Sometimes his shirts would get so stiff with salt from perspiration that they would break where they were wrinkled. There was never any money for more than bare necessities and as he was considered about the least important of the family, he either had to take what was left or do without. The other members of his family were so occupied with their own desires and affairs that they did not pay any attention to him, so he lived to himself. His mother was very kind and sympathetic but she was burdened with care of the smaller children and could not take up any time with him. The only real friend he had was Grace and her family objected to her associating with him because of the difference in the social standing of the two families. He liked to read and learn about things outside of his little world on the farm. One day he was reading a farm journal and he saw an advertisement that said if he would sell twelve subscriptions he could get a 22 rifle free. He slipped out one day and walked for miles across the prairie to the neighboring farm and sold the subscriptions. He received the rifle through the mail before his family knew anything about it. High Pocket's older brothers agreed to buy him some ammunition if he would let them shoot the rifle. High Pockets was mighty proud of his little rifle. He had heard so many stories about his pioneer ancestors who were expert riflemen, that he felt like owning a rifle was a big step toward becoming a man. He experienced for the first time the pleasure that goes with accomplishment. He spent many happy hours hunting and would come in from every trip loaded down with game. He became such a good shot with the little rifle that he could put a row of matches in a crack in the top plank of a board fence and light them without breaking the match stems. He would put empty 22 rifle shells on the ends of peach tree limbs and shoot them off without missing a shot. The Jack Rabbits were considered pests because they would destroy acres of cotton and gardens. The Farm Organizations offered to pay for every pair of rabbit ears brought in. High Pockets brought in rabbits ears by the sack full. (That was his first spending money.) High Pockets' parents began to realize that he and his little rifle were worth something to the family as the game he brought in helped to furnish the family table and he was making himself some money out of the bounty on rabbit ears, as well as helping to thin out the rabbits, so they let him have as much time off from work as they could. High Pockets' father always kept a pack of greyhounds to run rabbits. Greyhounds can run faster than any other kind of a dog, but they can't trail something. So he kept an old potlicker hound to trail the rabbits up. They called the old potlicker King. They had three greyhounds, Fido, Bruno, and Spot. Fido was fast as lightning for a short run but if he did not catch his rabbit right away he gave out and had to quit the race. Spot was short legged and could not keep up with Bruno, but he was long winded and was always pretty close behind when the race began to slow down, and when the rabbit began to dodge when Bruno got to crowding him too close, he would nearly always dodge right into Spot and he would be the one to match the catch. Bruno was a beautiful long legged blue greyhound. He was both the fastest and longest winded dog in the whole country, but he was bad to run over the rabbit when it got to dodging. High Pockets spent many happy days with his pack of hounds and his little rifle. When they would start out across the prairie the three greyhounds would trail along behind old King, who would nose his way through the grass for the scent of a rabbit trail. When he struck a hot trail he would let out a yelp that would echo across the hills and the whole pack would start jumping high into the air. Pretty soon the rabbit would jump out of his hiding place in the grass, the greyhounds would take charge and the race would be on. Jackrabbits usually run in a circle of about a mile. They nearly always circle to the right, and would come right back by where they started from. High Pockets would find a high place from which to watch the race as it made the circle. It was a thrilling experience to watch the rabbits bounding over the prairie lickety-split, with his ears laid flat running for dear life, while Bruno made a blue streak crowding at his heels. As the rabbit started back on the homestretch Highpockets watched closely to determine their course so that he would be in a position to shoot the rabbit as it came by. When it came within range of his rifle he would daw a bead on it and pull the trigger. The rabbit would be traveling so fast that it would look like a wheel rolling as the momentum carried it end over end for several feet after it was shot. In attempting to get rid of the rabbits the farmers would organize rabbit drives. The whole community would gather with their guns and form a line across the prairie. They would walk abreast of each other in line and cover the ground for miles around. There would be people from the surrounding towns,

Merchants, Bankers, and others that came for the sport. There would be an assortment of guns. Some of the men from the towns would have expensive guns. A cash prize was given to the one who killed the greatest number of rabbits. Highpockets had never been permitted to go on a rabbit drive because it was a rule that every one must have a gun, so now that he had a gun he felt qualified to go and when the line formed he fell in at the end of it, right by a big banker who had a shiney high powered gun. The people began to laugh and point at Highpockets with his little rifle, walking along beside the big banker with his expensive gun. The banker looked down at Highpockets with a sneer and asked him what he thought he could kill with that "Pea Shooter." But as they marched on side by side the rabbits began to jump up here and there. Highpockets could see a puff of smoke shoot out of each gun until the rabbit would quit running and start rolling. It was a rule that the man nearest the rabbit should have the first shot. If he missed then the next man down the line shot, and so on until the rabbit was killed. When the rabbit ran out away from the line it was easy to hit, but if it ran parallel with the line the man on the end of the line would usually be the first to get a shot at it because the others did not have room to shoot without shooting too close to the other men down the line. Highpockets was on the left end of the line and when a rabbit came his way he had a clear field and plenty of time to draw a bead, so he seldom missed his rabbit and to the dismay of all those whole poked fun at his "Pea Shooter" and the constarnation of the big banker with his high priced gun, Highpockets came in with the most rabbits killed on the drive. He received $25.00 in prize money and a considerable amount for the rabbit ears. He did not get very much recognition for having accomplished this feat as the other members of the hunt seemed to resent such an insignificant person taking the prize money. But he was accustomed to being snubbed so he did not expect anything else. He laughed to himself as he hid his money in an empty horse medicine can, on a rafter in the top of the loft. He felt that it would be safe there as he was the one that always had to climb up in the loft to throw down hay. This was the beginning of Highpockets' savings account which saved the ranch in the years to come.

CHAPTER III

As time passed Highpockets mused on the things of life, and wondered about things he did not understand. He lived close to nature, as he spent most of his time either strolling across prairies among the birds and animals or working in the field planting and cultivating growing things. He liked to watch the Sun rise. It resembled a great ball of fire rising out of the earth. He would watch it slowly rise through the haze of the horizon until it got too bright to look at. The West Texas Prairie is one of nature's most beautiful flower gardens. The Prairie Rose makes a pink carpet on which nature works a design with blue sweet williams, yellow butter cups, white daisies, orange pricklypear blossoms in one layer, and the rich white velvety blossoms of the flap mixed with golden rod and sunflower in another layer. It was always a great mystery to Highpockets why the sunflower always kept its face turned toward the sun. The prairie was teeming with all kinds of wild life. One thing that puzzled Highpockets most was why there was so much fighting among the animals, birds, and insects. Everyone of them had an enemy that he had to watch constantly to keep from being devoured. The old ringtailed hawk would fly low and hunt from the air. You would see him glide along for sometime then he would let his flaps and landing gear down for a quick landing and come up with a baby rabbit or a wriggling snake in his claws. The Blue Darter Hawk was the worst enemy to baby chicks and turkeys. He could dart into the barnyard, snatch up a baby chick and be gone before you could move. The sparrow hawk preyed on young birds and eggs in the nest. Every way Highpockets looked he could see fighting in the air and on the ground. The crow and the Ringtail Hawk were always having trouble.

The Hawk roosted in an old cotton wood tree down by the creek, and the crows roosted in a dead live oak out on the prairie. When the Hawk happened to fly too close to the Crow's home base, out he would come cawing and cursing, and they would start circling. The Crow would climb until he got altitude on the Hawk and down he'd come on his tail. The Hawk would let out a scream as the Crow yanked out a beak full of feathers. This would keep up until the Hawk was chased out of sight. The Crow was master over everything except the harmless little Scissored Tail Bird, who would do him just like he did the Hawk. The old Horned Toad would sprall on an ant hill and gobble up red ants until he was so full he could hardly wabble. The Spider would spin his web on the broom weeds and catch the flies, and the mud dobber would dip down and pick up the spider and fly away to his mud house where he would seal him in for winter food. The Diamond Back Rattle Snake was the most dreaded enemy of everything on the prairie, but he met his nemesis in the King Snake. That was one fight that always made Highpockets' knees shake to watch. There is something about the sound of rattle snake rattlers that chills the spine, and to stand in the tall grass and watch those two giant reptiles battle to the death made Highpockets wish he was somewhere else. Even the Bulls who graze together peacefully all through the winter would get mad at each other in the spring and go on a rampage. When they fought it was a blood curdling sight. Highpockets would hear the Mooeeow of one bull away off across the prairie, and pretty soon he would hear another one start up with the mumble mumble Mooeeow from another direction, and then they would be getting nearer, and then he would see them walking toward each other, slowly at first and then they would start trotting, and then running. All the time both of them screeching and bellowing so loud they could be heard for miles. Then they would stop a short distance apart and start pawing up dirt. They would lower their heads and start circling, getting closer and closer together each time, until finally one would lunge at the other with all his might and rip his flank with his horns, and the fight would be on. The sound of horns clashing together, and the thudding of heady bodies against each other as the bellowing blood splattered bulls fought to the finish was a hair raising experience. Highpockets also had an enemy he had to watch. There was an Old Yellow Maverick Bull, that would run everyone he found on foot. One day he spied Highpockets and took after him. Highpockets made for the nearest live oak tree and just as he reached the first limb the old maverick's head butted the tree right below his feet. The old maverick went around and around the tree pawing up dirt and snorting. It began to look like he was never going to leave so Highpockets shot him in the nose with his rifle and he took off like the heal flies were after him.

CHAPTER IV

The land Highpockets helped to cultivate was very poor. It was hillside land that had been planted to cotton for years, and erosion had cut great ditches in it. The surface soil had been washed away and quite often the plow he was breaking ground with would hang on a hitch rock, which would stall his team. He would have to work the plow loose and start out again. He decided that there was no point in leaving the rocks in the ground and having to pull the plow loose from them everytime the ground was plowed, so he got a crowbar and pick and carried them on the plow. Everytime he would hang his plow on a hitch rock he would dig the dirt from around it with the pick and pry it out of the ground with the crowbar. This was his own idea and he did not tell anyone he was doing it. When he finished breaking the land his father came out to look over the field and asked him where in the world all the rocks came from. Highpockets told him what he had done and his father made him get a team and wagon and haul the rocks out of the field. This was hard work and he wished many times before he had finished he had left the rocks in the ground, but the job was finally finished and all he got out of it was a lot of razzing from the other members of the family for getting himself a hard job. When he began hauling the rocks the idea occurred to him that if he piled them in the big ditch that had been washed out under the fence between the field and the pasture, it might stop the rain from washing all the soil out of the field and would fill up the hole under the fence so that when the next spring crop was planted the fence would not have to be repaired to keep out the livestock. (This was the beginning of soil conservation programme that helped reclaim hundreds of acres of land that had been devastated by erosion.) Highpockets enjoyed tilling the soil. Breaking the land was the easiest work there was to be done on the farm. All that had to be done was to sit on a plow, adjust a lever now and then to regulate the depth of the two big discs and set the guide wheel which kept the plow in the furrow, and to pull up on the lines at the corners and swing the four big miles around and back into the furrow again. It was monotonous work for anyone who did not enjoy the things of nature, but Highpockets could ride the plow for hours and hours watching the black dirt roll over. He always had company as the meadow larks and black birds would follow along behind the plow to feed on the bugs and worms in the fresh plowed ground. Babe would also stay around close to him while he was plowing. She would run and play all over the field, as if she were trying to get Highpockets to leave the plow and come out to play with her. It was while running across the field that she discovered she could pace. One day she started out with her neck bowed, fairly flying across the field. Her stocking legged feet moving in unison as if the front and back foot on each side were joined together, she never broke into a gallop but yet she was moving as fast as if she were running. Highpockets carried a long blacksnake whip on his plow, which he used to speed up a lazy mule. He practiced popping it and cutting twigs from the cotton stalks. He had a lot of fun with his whip. He could pop it so loud it would sound like the explosion of a gun. He could knock a horsefly off a mule's back and never move a hair on the mule. When he plowed up a snake he would bring the blacksnake whip up and slash its head off before it could get away. When a cotton tail rabbit rolled out from under the plow he would throw a half hitch around its neck and catch it with his whip. When time came to plant the crop that spring the planters and cultivators were put in condition. It had always been necessary to put wooden pegs in the covering plows on the planters because they would hang on the hitch rocks and bend if they had bolts in them. By using wooden pegs the pegs would break and the plow would flip over on the rock without being damaged. It was easier to replace a broken peg than to repair a bent plow. This made it necessary to make a lot of pegs. So, the pegs were made and everything made ready for the planting. When planting got under way everything went along fine, and no one noticed they had not broken a peg until the planting was finished, and all but Highpockets wondered why they did not strike any rocks.

CHAPTER V

There was an old well down on the creek which was surrounded by Cotton Wood Trees. This old well had not had any water in it for years according to the old settlers, but at one time it never went dry even during time of drought. That was before all the land above it was put into cultivation and permitted to wash away. Highpockets spent a great deal of his time during the hot summer months lounging around on the green grass under the cotton wood trees. After two summers had passed Babe had grown to be a beautiful fillie. She was very gentle and followed Highpockets every where he went but he had never tried to ride her. He decided it was about time he broke her to ride, so one day while they were looking at the old well he swung himself up across her back. This was something new to Babe, as nothing had ever been on her back before. In her shock from the strange experience, instinct got the upperhand of her reasoning and she flew into the air bucking with all her might until Highpockets came tumbling down on his face on the ground. This was the first time Highpockets had really been mad enough to be rough with Babe, but when he got up and rubbed his hand over his face, and found it bleeding and thought about how the family would raz him about getting thrown by his baby, he made up his mind that he was going to ride Babe home that night. He took his knife and cut a piece off the end of his lairet rope long enough to make a surrysingle. He threw it across her back and girted it up tight. He then took the halter rope in his left hand and got hold of the surrysingle with his right hand and swung across her back again. Babe stood perfectly still for a few minutes, not knowing just what to think, but again the impulse took hold of her and she left the ground again with all four feet. Around and around they went with Highpockets hanging to the surrysingle with all his might, but finally after completely exhausting herself Babe gave up and walked along just as if she had been used to someone riding her all the time. Highpockets' spirits rose higher that evening than they had ever been before as he rode home on his beautiful gold-en colored Babe. By this time Highpockets had saved enough money from his income from bounty on rabbit ears and hides of varmints he had sold, to buy him a saddle and bridle. So he went to Hico with his father one day and brought back a saddle and bridle just the color of Babe. After Babe got used to the feel of the saddle on her back she took as much pride in racing across the hills and meadows as Highpockets did. By this time Grace had learned to ride the big blue roan that her father had given her and they would meet at the old well and ride for hours together. As horse racing was the main sport on the ranch their first thought of fun on horses was to run a race. So they decided to canter to a big cottonwood tree, giving the horses their heads at that point they raced down the level floor of the valley. Babe had trouble getting started. She did not want to run, but finally she managed to get both front feet off the ground at the same time and broke into a dead run, but the long legged blue roan had gotten so far ahead that she never was able to catch up. While riding, Grace and Highpockets had noticed that while the blue roan galloped along with that rocking chair gallop of his, Babe would always keep along side of him by swinging into the racking gate she liked so well. It was a beautiful picture to watch the feet of these two horses. It resembled the synchronized action of the drive wheel and shaft on a speeding locomotive. The smooth circular motion of Blue's galloping feet criss crossed by the horizontal movement back and forth of Babe's perfectly timed pacing. Both animals moving so smoothly that their riders looked as though they were glued to their saddles. Babe could pace faster than Blue could run. The two horses responded to different starting signals. Blue would spring into action when Grace would slack up on the reins and lean forward in the saddle, but Babe would shoot forward like a rocket when Highpockets pulled up tight on the reins and sat back in the saddle. While on their daily rides Grace and Highpockets taught their horses to do tricks. They would make Blue and Babe rear up and walk on their hind feet, and while standing up this way they would walk up and shake hands with each other like people do. Highpockets would get on Blue behind Grace's saddle, and they would make Blue jump over Babe, and Highpockets would slide off Blue as he went over the land in the saddle of Babe. Highpockets would hook his legs around the horn of the saddle and swing himself down under Babe while he was running: catch a hold of the stirrup on the other side, swing himself under her, pull himself up to where he could reach the horn of the saddle and swing into the saddle on the other side, without stopping. He practiced doing rope tricks with his lariat rope. He would twirl a rope around both horses while they were running and make them jump through it. One of his best tricks was to have the horses run past each other in opposite directions and both of them jump through the loop as they passed each other. It was while the owner of the saddle horse breeding farm was bird hunting with the owner of the ranch, that he first saw Babe and discovered that she could pace faster than Blue could run. He told the owner of the ranch to have her brought to his farm and they would train her to work to a cart, which was the type of rig used in training pacing horses. Up to this time no one had seemed to be interested in Babe but Highpockets and Grace, but now that she was noticed by the owner of the fastest pacing horse in the county everyone sat up and took notice of her.

The landlord told Highpockets' father that since Babe had been raised on his farm and had been fed his feed that he should be allowed to have an interest in her. Highpockets' father feared that if he did not let the landlord have his say about everything, he might make them move off the land, so he told Highpockets that they would have to take Babe back to the landlord. This was the hardest blow Highpockets had ever been dealt. He climbed up in the loft and buried his head in the loose hay and cried his heart out. He spent a lot of his time up there in his hideout all alone with his grief. It was while he was hiding up there one day that one of his brothers found him, counting his money and discovered that he kept it hid up there. Highpockets knew that he could no longer use the loft for a hiding place, so he took his money down to the old well. The old well was curbed with stones and since it had gone dry it had been partly filled up so that by tying a rope to a willow tree by the side of the well he could let himself down to the dry bottom with safety. He climbed down the rope and pulled out a loose rock at the bottom. He then pushed the medicine can containing the money in the hole in the curb, after digging out enough dirt to make room for it behind the rock and pushed the rock back in the hole. Hiding his money here was what caused him later to discover that the old well had water in it, and saved the livestock on the ranch during a terrible drought.

CHAPTER VI

Highpockets was so despondent over the prospects of having to give Babe up, that he could not eat. He would not talk to anyone, not even to Grace. He lost weight and the family became alarmed for fear he would become seriously ill. Grace and Highpockets' mother were drawn together by their mutual interest in him, and they decided that they must if at all possible do something about it, so they enlisted the help of Grace's mother and three of them managed to persuade the landlord to permit Highpockets to keep Babe between training periods. The only means of transportation available at that time was either horse drawn vehicles or on horse back. The nearest Doctor was twelve miles away. On a stormy night in April of that year Highpockets' mother took suddenly ill. The first thought in the minds of the family was to get a Doctor as quickly as possible and as there were no telephones the only way to get one was to go get him. While the other members of the family were discussing who would go and how they would go, Highpockets slipped out the back door and ran down to the barn. He threw the saddle on Babe and swung himself into it. Riding up to the plank gate he slid the latch back, rode through and closed it it behind him. As he rode past the front yard gate his father came out with his oldest brother heading for the barn. Highpockets did not slow up, but yelled into the roaring thunder that he was going. Down the narrow lane they flew guided away from the barbed wire fence on each side only by the constant flashing of sheet lightning. The heavy black cloud rolled on toward them and they could see angry looking green whirlpools in it when a jagged streak of lightning would race across it. He had just reached the end of the narrow lane that lead out into the main road when the first drops of rain began to fall.
He felt safer on the main road because there was no longer any danger of crashing Babe into the barbed wires that lined the

narrow lane. In his haste he forgot his hat and coat and when the onslaught of the storm hit he was drenched to the skin with the first rain that fell. He did not feel any discomfort, however, as the feverish excitement numbed his senses to everything except the desire to get to the Doctor. He crouched low over Babe's neck so that her flying mane would shield his face from the stinging rain. He wrapped a bridle rein around each hand so that the wet leather would not slip through his fingers and held Babe's head steady as he coaxed her on through the storm. The rhythmic clop clop of the sure footed Babe's feet falling on the hard packed earth accompanied by the screeching of saddle leather was music in his ears as he went sailing through the rain. Highpockets was so absorbed in his thoughts that it did not seem he had been long on the road when he saw the lights of the town to which he was going. By the time he got to the River Bridge on the street leading into town, water was gushing under it in torrents. He swung Babe onto the bridge and as they crossed it the boards rattled and the iron turnbuckles that were used to brace the structure banged together as the bridge swayed. Highpockets had no difficulty in reaching his destination, as everybody in the County knew where old Doc Ridinghower lived. He had the finest home in the town. It was a big two story white house with huge colonial style pillows in front of it and sat upon the highest hill anywhere around. He rang the door bell and was met at the door by the Doctor's wife who asked him in. When he told her his story she immediately obtained some wraps for him and went up stairs to call the Doctor. He was one of those saintly old country doctors who never considered himself until the patients' needs were taken care of. So he set about making preparations for the trip out to the farm. While he was dressing, his wife awoke the stable boy and gave him instructions to harness the fastest horses in the stable. The Doctor traveled in a buggy pulled by two of the best harness horses that could be obtained. His fastest team was a perfectly matched pair of red-roan mares. They were full sisters. There was only one years difference in their ages. They were gaited exactly alike and could make buggy wheels sing when they dashed down the road as their long legs reach out from under the breast yoke in their long gated trot. The Doctor put Highpockets in the buggy with him and they led Babe behind the buggy. Everything went along smoothly until they came to Duffau Creek which was about a mile from the farm. When they got to the creek the bridge was under water, so they could not cross in the buggy, so they went back to a farm house they had just passed and left the Doctor's rig. The Doctor put Highpockets in bed at the neighbor's house and got on Babe with his medicine kit and swam her across the creek. He was hardly able to get his mind on his patient for singing the praise of Babe and Highpockets. The seriousness of his mother's illness occupied the minds of Highpockets' family for several weeks and his heroic trip after the Doctor was soon forgotten. Babe had become so famous that the landlord realized she was a very valuable mare and when Highpockets' father went to him to borrow money with which to pay the doctor bill, he told him he would not give him the loan but would pay him $500.00 for his interest in Babe, which would take care of the bill. After having a secret agreement with Grace that she would not let her father sell Babe to anyone else, Highpockets consented to let her go. It hurt like rip to see Babe being handled by the ruthless trainers, but he consoled himself with the knowledge that Grace would take good care of her, and he resolved to save all the money he could so he could some day buy her back. It did not make him feel very good either when he watched Babe win race after race and win the landlord enough prize money to have enabled Highpockets to buy a good farm had he been able to keep her.

CHAPTER VII

The rain that came the night Highpockets' mother became ill washed the loose soil out of the field. The seeds that had been planted were ruined and the crop had to be replanted. As Highpockets' brothers drove into the field they noticed that where the big ditch had gone under the fence before Highpockets piled the rocks in it, there was several acres of black level land. The rocks had caught the soil as it washed from the hillside above, and instead of going on down the creek it had fanned out and settled inside the field to form a layer of rich soil. The crop was replanted and this time they got a good stand. As time passed the cotton grew and began to put on small squares; then white blooms began to appear, and in a few days they turned purple and finally dried up and fell off and tiny green balls appeared which grew to be the size of a hen egg and then popped open to make fluffy white balls. No one noticed any difference in the cotton until time came to harvest the crop. When picking time came and they went into the field with their sacks, they discovered that the stalks on the five acres of fresh made land were much taller and their sacks got full a lot quicker than they did on the land above it. All that was said about it that year was just to comment on how much more cotton grew on the patch down by the old well place than any other part of the field. Highpockets knew in his own mind what had caused the land to produce, although he had long ago learned that there was no point in his expressing his opinion as he was either laughed down by his older brothers or ridiculed by his father, but he got a lot of secret satisfaction out of what he knew he had done. The school he attended organized a corn club that winter. He joined the club and persuaded his father to let him plant an acre of corn down by the old well place. He produced more corn on his acre than was produced on any other acre on the whole ranch. Following instructions given to him in school he planted peas and pumpkins in the corn the last plowing before laying it by, and besides making the most corn he raised enough peas and pumpkins to supply the whole neighborhood. He also won a $10.00 prize which was offered by the banker whom he had beat shooting Jack Rabbits, for the best 10 ears of corn exhibited at the old settlers reunion that fall. A drought set in that summer about the time the corn was ready to harvest. For several months it did not rain a drop. Wells began going dry and stock water was getting scarce. It began to look as through the cattle on the ranch would starve for water. When Highpockets went down in the old well to put away his prize money he had won for the best ten ears of corn, he noticed that it was damp down there. When he pulled the old horse medicine can out it had moisture on it. He dug some of the rocks up from the bottom of the well and found water under them. Highpockets' mind began to race. He sat down and tried to figure out what had happened. Here it was the dryest weather in years but yet there was water in the bottom of the old well. He decided he had better not hide his money down there anymore so he took it out and started back to the house. On his way to the house he met the landlord and the banker. The drought had ruined the grass on the range and the landlord was trying to get a loan from the banker with which to buy feed for his herds. The banker had come out to look over the cattle that were to be used as collateral for the loan. Highpockets was so excited over his discovery that he forgot his usual shyness in the presence of these big men and told them in choking syllables that there was water in the old well. The landlord laughed at him and said it was impossible, as there had never been water in that old well since he had owned the ranch. But curiosity got the best of the Banker and he asked Highpockets to show him the water. Highpockets led the way down to the old well. He climbed down in it and raised up a rock. There was water where the rock had been. He took the money out of the old can and put it in his pocket. He then dipped up some water in the old can and tied it on the end of the rope, and the banker pulled it up. He took the can off and dropped the rope back in the well so Highpockets could climb out. When he climbed out the landlord and the banker were sitting on the well curb scratching their heads. The banker began looking at High-pockets, as if he was seeing him for the first time. This little slip of a boy who had beat him shooting with a little old pea shooter of a rifle and had beat all the good farmers in the country raising corn on land that had been so poor it had never raised corn before, had pulled another rabbit out of the hat by finding water in a well that had been dry for years, in the driest year anyone could remember. He began to ask Highpockets questions. Highpockets was so choked and embarrassed he could hardly talk. No one had ever considered his opinion worth asking for before and especially the big banker. The banker asked him how he produced his corn. After Highpockets found his tongue so he could talk he began to tell just what he did to the corn. The landlord pointed to the patch just across the fence from the old well and suggested that the three of them walk out in it. As they waded through the tangle of dead corn stalks, pea and pumpkin vines tangled in among the tall crab grass that had grown up since the crop was layed by they began to see what happened. The land lord stopped suddenly as if something had hit him full in the face. He began to look up and down the fence. He discovered the rocks piled high where the ditch formerly was. He saw that the soil had washed nearly up to the top of the rocks. He then asked Highpockets where the rocks came from. This question was too much for Highpockets, as he was filled with welled up emotions that his chin began to tremble. He finally regained his composure and began unraveling the story about how he had gotten tired of pulling the plow loose from the hitch rocks and dug them up, hauled them out of the field and piled them in the ditch along the fence and how after seeing how much more cotton grew on the new made land that he chose that for his acre of corn. While Highpockets was talking to the landlord, the banker was studying the landscape with his subconscious mind while listening to the conversation. As he pondered over the situation realization came to his mind with a jolt, as to the significance of what Highpockets had done. He was so aroused by this realization that he could hardly wait for Highpockets to finish his story. When Highpockets had finished his story the banker turned to the landlord and said, "I have read in the scripture where is says 'and a small child will lead them.' This little boy has shown me just what this whole country needs to know. By piling those rocks in the ditch he caught the soil that was washing away. The new made soil grew a dense growth of vegetation which not only caught more soil but also held the water so that it soaked into the ground on the water shed above the old well, and now that water is seeping into the well and we will have water for our livestock." The banker told the landlord he could have his loan with which to feed his cattle through the drought. The three of them started back to the ranch house. The banker caught Highpockets by the hand and pulled him up on the horse behind him. As Highpockets swung up, his money fell out of his pocket. The banker got down and retrieved it for him and asked what he was doing carrying his money around with him. After Highpockets told him his reason, the banker told him that if he would put it in his bank he would add $100.00 to it if he would start a saving account.

When they reached the farm house the landlord told their story to Highpockets' father, who immediately told his other boys to go down and clean out the old well. For the first time in his life he got to set by and watch someone else do the dirty work. They cleaned all the rocks and trash out of the well, then got a big bucket and dipped up the mud. After digging about ten feet they found a smooth sand rock curb around the well, and the mud gave way to white water sand. By the time they got down twenty feet the water was pouring in faster than they could draw it out so they climbed out of the well stripped off their muddy clothes and began pouring buckets of clear cool water over each other to clean off the mud. They were all having a jolly good time until they saw all the women coming across the prairie to look at the well, and they had to grab up their clothes and run for cover among the willow trees. The rancher felt under obligation to Highpockets since he had pulled him out of a tight spot, so he told him that if he would move over to the ranch house he would pay him the same salary he was paying his top hands. After talking it over with his parents it was agreed that he should go. He did not want to leave his mother, but his loss of love for his brothers outweighed by the satisfaction he was getting out of being able to lord it over them after so many years of their bossing him around. He was very uncomfortable at first in his new surroundings. He had always lived in an old two room shotgun house with a lean-to on the side of it. It was so crowded with beds that there was barely room to walk between them. The furniture consisted of half a dozen iron beds, one old fashioned dresser, a few cowhide bottom straight chairs and two old hickory bark rocking chairs. In the lean-to which was used for a dining room and kitchen there was a big wood cook stove with an old fashioned cupboard and a long dinner table covered with oil cloth with benches on each side of it for seats and a small cook table. There was no plumbing fixtures. Water had to be carried from the well for house use. There was a bench outside the back door with tin wash basins on it which were used for shaving and washing up for meals. When they bathed they would heat water in a big iron wash pot in the back yard and bath in a wash tub in the smoke house. Highpockets felt so out of place in the big ranch house he could hardly eat his meals. There were so many halls and rooms that he thought he would never find his way around. Every room had beautiful rugs and fine furniture, and the walls were lined with beautiful paintings and pictures of all the ancestors as well as the present members of the family. The dining room was nicely furnished with tables and chairs. The tables were covered with clean white linen. There was beautifully designed silver and china dishes that had pretty flowers painted on them. They were so thin that Highpockets was afraid to touch them for fear of breaking them. There was a cabinet at one end of the dining room which was filled with crystal that reflected thousands of tiny lights from the flare of the carbide lights which were suspended from the ceiling of the dining room. It all seemed like a dream to Highpockets as he had never seen anything like it before. Highpockets was given a room all to himself. It was nicely furnished with a dresser, two chairs, and library table, a wash stand with a china bowl and pitcher, and clean white towels hanging on a rack on the back of it. The bed had clean white linen on it and the feather mattress was so soft it felt like he was floating on air. He was also permitted to eat with the family. The other ranch hands resented this and some of them were very jealous of him, but were afraid to let on as they knew they would get fired. Highpockets and Grace spent many happy days riding Babe and Blue over the big ranch together.

THE END

Finding Your Ancestors

Introduction (Connie)

My interest in genealogy began when I was in third grade. My teacher, Miss Esterbrook assigned us the task of creating a family tree. At that time, my only resource was Mamie, my paternal grandmother. Fortunately, she provided a wealth of information which included photos and hand-written postcards from the early 1900s. Since we lived in the house my great grandparents built, there was also an old red velvet photo album and a very large family Bible tucked away in a window seat. Both provided more information. And finally, we visited two cemeteries. My grandfather's family (going back three generations) was buried in the first cemetery and my grandmother's parents were buried in the second cemetery. Now, we can simply go to "find a grave" online.

Twenty years later, my dad, my brother, and I sat around the kitchen table to discuss what we thought might be our family tree. People who could have told us the first-hand stories were now gone. We only had our memories to draw upon and they were very sparse. We wrote what we knew (or thought we knew) on a series of napkins taped together to build the first draft of our tree. We divided the old photos. Half to my brother and half to me. And we vowed that he and I would research and share our family history.

Since that first assignment in third grade, the availability of tools and resources is incredible. For example, instead of walking through the cemetery looking at headstones you can use www.findagrave.com and many other online tools to find your ancestors. More about that later.

Validate Your Research

We suggest you validate your family tree through rigorous research. It might be easy to look at existing paper or online family trees and assume they are correct. However, if your goal is to ensure that the family tree you create and the one you leave behind for future generations is correct, then we encourage you to validate your work.

Here are some suggestions for validating your research:
- Hire and or work with professionals from your local and state genealogy associations. (e.g. Texas State Genealogical Societ txsgs.org)
- Work with a certified genealogist from a professional board such as the Board for Certification of Genealogists (BCG) or the International Commission for the Accreditation of Professional Genealogists (ICAPGen)
- Volunteer at the state and local level to find resources and meet new friends
- Use original documents such as birth certificates, marriage records, census records, and land records to validate your research
- Cross-reference data from multiple sources will help confirm accuracy
- DNA testing such as Ancestry or 23andMe also provide additional confirmation of relationships

Validating genealogy family trees involves cross-referencing information from multiple reliable sources such as birth certificates, marriage records, census data, church records, military records, and other historical documents. It's essential to verify information from primary sources whenever possible and to be cautious of errors or discrepancies in secondary sources.

Collaborating with other genealogists, using genealogy software with built-in validation features, and seeking guidance from professional genealogists can also help ensure the accuracy of family trees.

Vital Records

Vital records refer to official documentation of major life events that are kept under governmental authority. They serve both as legal documents and essential resources for various purposes, including genealogical research, legal proceedings, and verifying personal information. Here's a breakdown of the main types of vital records:

1. Birth Certificates
- Description: An official document recording the birth of an individual.
- Details Included: Full name of the person, date and place of birth, names of parents, the attending physician, and often the parents' ages, occupations, and places of birth.

2. Death Certificates
- Description: An official document recording the death of an individual.
- Details Included: Full name of the deceased, date and place of death, cause of death, burial details, the attending physician, often information about the deceased's parents and spouse, and sometimes additional information like the deceased's occupation and place of birth.

3. Marriage Certificates/Licenses
- Description: Official documentation of the union between two individuals.
- Details Included: Names of the individuals getting married, date and place of marriage, names of witnesses, and often the names of the parents of the bride and groom. A marriage license grants permission for a marriage to take place, while a marriage certificate provides proof that the ceremony occurred.

4. Divorce Decrees/Records
- Description: Official documentation of the dissolution of a mar-

riage.

- Details Included: Names of the individuals involved, date and place of the marriage, date and place of the divorce, the reason for the divorce, terms of property division, child custody arrangements, and other relevant details.

Other Vital Records:

- Civil Union and Domestic Partnership Records: Similar to marriage records but pertain to other officially recognized unions.
- Adoption Records: Document the legal adoption of a child. Access to these records may be restricted to protect the privacy of those involved.

Importance of Vital Records:

- Legal Evidence: They serve as official proof of an event. For instance, a birth certificate is often required to obtain a passport, while a marriage certificate might be required for spousal benefits.
- Genealogical Research: Vital records are fundamental resources for individuals tracing their family history.
- Statistical Analysis: Governments and organizations use aggregated data from vital records for public health studies, policy-making, and population statistics.
- Identity Verification: These records are used to confirm an individual's identity in various circumstances, such as applying for jobs, joining the military, or obtaining other official documents.

Access to Vital Records:

- Availability: While many vital records are public documents, access to certain records, especially more recent ones, may be restricted to protect individuals' privacy. Over time, older records often become more accessible to the public.
- Storage: Vital records are typically stored by government agencies, such as departments of health, vital statistics offices, or county courthouses.

- Digitization: Many vital records have been digitized and are available online, making it easier for researchers and the general public to access them. Websites like Ancestry.com, FamilySearch.org, and local government databases often host such records.

In summary, vital records are official documents that record significant life events. They play a crucial role in both legal proceedings and personal matters, such as genealogical research.

Professional Genealogy

Professionally certified genealogists can offer valuable assistance in validating your genealogy research in several ways:

1. Expertise: Certified genealogists possess specialized knowledge and skills in conducting thorough research, analyzing evidence, and interpreting historical records.

2. Verification of Sources: They can help verify the accuracy and reliability of sources you've used in your research, ensuring that you're basing your findings on credible information.

3. Correcting Errors: Certified genealogists can identify and correct any errors or discrepancies in your research, providing a more accurate depiction of your family history.

4. Access to Records: They may have access to resources and archives that are not readily available to the general public, which can be instrumental in uncovering additional information about your ancestors.

5. Methodological Guidance: They can provide guidance on research methodologies and best practices, helping you navigate complex genealogical puzzles and break through brick walls in your research.

6. Peer Review: Certified genealogists often engage in peer review processes, where they collaborate with other professionals to evaluate and critique each other's work, ensuring the highest standards of accuracy and integrity.

Overall, collaborating with certified genealogists can enhance the quality and reliability of your genealogy research, providing you with a more comprehensive understanding of your family's heritage.

Association of Professional Genealogists

The Association of Professional Genealogists (APG) is an international organization dedicated to supporting professional genealogists in all aspects of their work. This organization plays a crucial role in setting standards for genealogical research and business practices within the field. Here are key aspects of the Association of Professional Genealogists:

- Membership and Scope: The APG's membership includes professional genealogists from around the world. Members offer a range of services, including family history research, forensic genealogy, lecturing, writing, and publishing in the field of genealogy.

- Professional Development: One of the APG's primary goals is to support the professional development of its members. This includes providing educational opportunities, resources, and mentoring for those who are developing their genealogical skills or building their businesses.

- Code of Ethics: The APG has a Code of Ethics and Professional Practices that its members are expected to adhere to. This code sets standards for responsible, ethical treatment of clients and their research needs, and it guides professionals in their work and interactions.

- Conferences and Learning Opportunities: The organization hosts conferences, webinars, and other events that provide opportunities for professional growth, networking, and staying updated on the latest developments in genealogy.

- Publications and Resources: The APG publishes materials beneficial to genealogists, including a quarterly magazine, a monthly newsletter, and various guides and resources relevant to genealogical research and business practices.
- Advocacy and Public Awareness: The APG works to raise public awareness about the value of genealogical research and the profession of genealogy. It also advocates for access to public records and other resources essential to genealogical research.
- Directory of Members: The APG provides an online directory of its members, making it easier for individuals and organizations to find professional genealogists who can assist with specific research needs or projects.
- Special Interest Groups: The APG hosts special interest groups for members focusing on particular areas of genealogy, offering a platform for sharing specialized knowledge and practices.

Overall, the Association of Professional Genealogists is instrumental in promoting high standards and ethical practices in genealogy, serving as a valuable resource for both professional genealogists and those seeking professional assistance in their genealogical research.

If you choose to work with a certified genealogist, here are some resources.

1. Board for Certification of Genealogists (BCG) - (Certified Genealogist CG)
PO Box 14291
Washington, DC 20044
https://www.BCGcertification.org

The Genealogy Standards Second Edition Revised by the Board for Certification of Genealogists includes standards for documentation, research, writing and other useful information.

2. International Commission for the Accreditation of Professional Genealogists (ICAPGen).(Accredited Genealogist AG)
P.O. Box 4464

Salt Lake City, UT. 84110-4464
ICAPGen.ORG

3. https://www.heritagebridge.com/blog/2022/3/9/accredited-genealogists-and-certified-genealogists-different-credentials-that-both-lead-to-quality-research

Genealogy Tools

You may have heard someone say "We don't know what we don't know." That is so true when we begin researching our family tree. Don't be surprised if you hear yourself saying "I can't believe my Dad or Mom never told me that."

So we suggest starting with what we do know and asking family members and friends what they know. Check out common and not-so common genealogy sites. Attend online and live training sessions. Join a local genealogy group or specialized organizations such as Sons or Daughters of the American Revolution.

There are numerous tools and resources available to those interested in genealogy, which is the study of family history and lineage. The best tools for you will depend on your specific needs, whether you're starting from scratch, need to organize data you already have, or are looking to connect with living relatives. Here is a list of some commonly used tools:

Online Databases and Services

- Ancestry.com: One of the most popular genealogical services, offering a huge database of public records and a user-friendly interface. Requires a subscription for full access.

- FamilySearch.org: Operated by The Church of Jesus Christ of Latter-day Saints, this website offers free access to a vast collection of records and is useful for building a family tree.

- MyHeritage: Similar to Ancestry.com, offers a searchable database and DNA testing.

- Findmypast: Particularly useful for those with British or Irish

46

ancestry, this service offers a lot of UK-specific databases.

- 23andMe, Living DNA, and other DNA services: These offer genetic testing to help you identify relatives and trace your ethnicity.

Software

- Gramps: An open-source genealogy program that offers a lot of customizable options.

- Family Tree Maker: Paid software that syncs with your Ancestry.com account to make it easy to update your family tree both online and offline.

- Legacy Family Tree: Another paid option with extensive charting capabilities and a comprehensive suite of tools.

Mobile Apps

- Ancestry Mobile App: For on-the-go access to your Ancestry.com account.

- MyHeritage Mobile App: Similar functionalities as its web version, but optimized for mobile use.

- FamilySearch Tree: Allows you to access the FamilySearch database from your mobile device.

Books, Magazines, and Other Resources

- Local libraries and archives: Many offer free access to genealogical databases and other local records.

- Genealogy-specific magazines: Titles like "Family Tree Magazine" offer tips, tricks, and the latest news in the field.

- Webinars and Online Courses: Websites like genealogy.com offer various courses, some of which are free, to hone your skills.

- Genealogical Societies: Local, national, and ethnicity-specific genealogical societies can offer unique resources, databases, and expertise.

Organizational Tools

- Evernote or OneNote: These general-purpose note-taking apps are great for organizing your research.

- Google Drive or Dropbox: Cloud storage solutions can help

you keep all of your research in one easily accessible place.

- Spreadsheets: Microsoft Excel or Google Sheets are useful for tracking records, dates, and other details.

Specialized Websites

- The USGenWeb Project: Useful for American genealogy, offering free access to a wealth of data.

- Cyndi's List: A comprehensive list of genealogy sites on the Internet, categorized & cross-referenced.

- Ellis Island Passenger Search: If your ancestors immigrated to the U.S., this database could prove helpful.

Remember, genealogy can be a complex task, so it's often useful to employ a combination of these resources to get a comprehensive understanding of your family history.

Ancestry.com

Ancestry.com is a commercial genealogical website that assists individuals in researching their family history and constructing their family tree. Below is a detailed description of Ancestry.com:
Overview

- Founded: Ancestry.com was established in 1983 as Ancestry Publishing, with its online presence launching in 1996.

- Headquarters: The company is based in Lehi, Utah, USA.

- Database: Ancestry.com boasts an extensive collection of records, including census, military, immigration, and vital records from many countries. As of September 2021, they claim to have over 27 billion records from more than 80 countries.

Key Features

- Searchable Records: Users can search through billions of historical records to find information about their ancestors, ranging from birth and death certificates to military service records and passenger lists.

- Family Trees: Users can create and maintain their own family tree, adding details and stories for each member. They can also attach historical records and photographs to individuals in their tree.

- DNA Testing: In addition to record-based genealogy, Ancestry.com offers DNA testing through AncestryDNA. This service allows users to explore their genetic roots, find DNA matches among other users, and even pinpoint geographic areas of origin for their ancestors.

- Ancestry Academy: This feature offers online courses that help users hone their genealogical research skills.

- Hints: As users add information to their family trees, Ancestry.com offers "hints" that suggest possible connections to historical records or other family trees, aiding in the research process.

- Mobile App: Ancestry.com has a mobile app that allows users to research on-the-go and view their family tree from their mobile devices.

- Collaboration: Users can collaborate with family members or other researchers, sharing their family trees and combining research efforts.

Membership and Pricing

- Ancestry.com operates on a subscription-based model. Free trials are often available, but to access most of the site's record collections and features, users need a paid subscription.

- There are different membership levels, each providing access to different sets of records. For instance, some memberships may focus on U.S. records, while others provide global access.

Conclusion

Ancestry.com is one of the leading resources for genealogical research and has played a significant role in popularizing genealogy among the general public. With its vast collection of records and innovative tools like DNA testing, it offers both novice and experienced genealogists a comprehensive platform to explore their family history.

MyHeritage

MyHeritage is an online genealogy platform that allows users to research their family history, create family trees, and explore their genetic ancestry through DNA testing. Here's a detailed description of MyHeritage:

Overview

- Founded: MyHeritage was founded in 2003 by Gilad Japhet.

- Headquarters: The company is headquartered in Or Yehuda, Israel.

- Database: MyHeritage has a vast collection of historical records, family tree profiles, and DNA data, making it one of the largest resources of its kind in the world. As of my last update in September 2021, the platform had over 13 billion historical records.

Key Features

- Family Tree Builder: MyHeritage offers a user-friendly tool that enables individuals to construct, visualize, and edit their family trees.

- Historical Records: Users can search through billions of records, including census data, birth, marriage and death certificates, military records, and more, from various countries around the world.

- Smart Matches™: When users upload or input their family trees, MyHeritage's Smart Matches™ technology automatically compares them to other trees on the platform and notifies users of potential family connections.

- DNA Testing: MyHeritage offers DNA testing services that provide insights into one's ethnic origins and potential DNA matches with relatives. Their test examines autosomal DNA, which includes information from both maternal and paternal lines.

- Photo Tools: The platform has introduced innovative photo tools such as MyHeritage In Color™, which colorizes black and white photos, and Deep Nostalgia™, which animates faces in still photos.

- Mobile App: MyHeritage has a mobile app that allows users to work on their family tree, view and upload photos, and get match notifications on-the-go.

Membership and Pricing

- MyHeritage operates with both free and subscription-based models. While anyone can create a basic family tree and access some features for free, full access to all historical records and advanced features requires a paid subscription.

- The DNA testing service is priced separately from the platform's subscription fee.

Privacy and Data Handling
MyHeritage emphasizes user privacy and has a strict policy against selling or sharing DNA data without explicit consent. They also provide the option for users to delete their DNA data permanently from their servers.
MyHeritage is a comprehensive genealogical platform that caters to both individuals interested in their family's history and those delving into genetic ancestry. With a combination of traditional genealogical research tools and innovative technological features, MyHeritage has made a significant mark in the world of family history exploration.

FamilySearch

FamilySearch is a free online genealogy service that provides access to a vast collection of records and resources for individuals researching their family history. It is operated by The Church of Jesus Christ of Latter-day Saints (LDS Church). Here's a detailed description of FamilySearch:
Overview

- Founded: The roots of FamilySearch can be traced back to the establishment of the Genealogical Society of Utah in 1894. The FamilySearch platform as we know it began its online presence in 1999.

- Headquarters: The main operations are based in Salt Lake City, Utah, USA, particularly at the Family History Library, one of the world's largest genealogical libraries.

- Database: FamilySearch boasts a massive collection of genealogical and historical records. As of September 2021, the platform claimed to have digitized billions of records from all over the world.

Key Features

- Searchable Records: FamilySearch offers users the ability to search through a vast collection of historical documents, including birth, marriage, and death records, censuses, probates, military records, and more.

- Family Tree: Users can create and manage their family tree on the platform. One unique aspect of FamilySearch's tree is that it's a collaborative tree, meaning users contribute to a shared global tree rather than maintaining individual trees.

- Research Wiki: The FamilySearch Research Wiki is a valuable tool for both novice and experienced genealogists. It offers articles, guides, and tips related to genealogical research in various countries and regions.

- Communities & Forums: The platform has communities and forums where users can ask questions, collaborate on research, and share insights.

- Learning Resources: FamilySearch provides various learning materials, including tutorials, courses, and webinars to assist users in their genealogical journey.

- Indexing: This volunteer-driven feature allows users to assist in making more records searchable by transcribing (or "indexing") the information from digitized records.

- Catalog & Books: FamilySearch offers a catalog of its vast collection of microfilms and books, many of which are digitized and accessible online.

- Mobile App: The FamilySearch Tree and FamilySearch Memories apps allow users to access and contribute to their family tree, as well as upload family photos and stories on-the-go.

Membership and Pricing

- Free Access: One of the distinguishing features of FamilySearch is that it's entirely free to use. The LDS Church funds it as a public service, so users don't need a subscription or payment to access its resources.

Privacy and Data Handling

- While FamilySearch allows users to add and manage information about their ancestors, there are privacy controls in place for living individuals. Details about living people are kept private and are only visible to the person who added them and to whom they give explicit permission.

FamilySearch is a comprehensive and free platform for genealogical research. With its roots in the longstanding genealogical efforts of the LDS Church, the platform provides tools, resources, and a vast collection of records that make it a vital resource for anyone interested in exploring their family history.

Legacy Family Tree

Legacy Family Tree is a genealogy software program used by family history enthusiasts to research, record, and share their genealogy. It's known for its comprehensive features that allow users to organize, document, and present their family history research. Here's a detailed description of Legacy Family Tree:

Overview

- Developed By: Millennia Corporation.

- Initial Release: The software has been around for several decades, with continuous updates and versions being released to accommodate the changing needs of genealogists and advances in technology.

Key Features

- Family View and Pedigree View: These are the main interfaces of the program, showing an individual's ancestors, descendants, or both, allowing for easy navigation through the family tree.

- Comprehensive Reporting: Users can produce a variety of reports, charts, and forms, such as pedigree charts, descendant reports, and family group sheets.

- Sources and Citations: Legacy places a strong emphasis on documenting sources. Users can easily add source citations to any fact or event in an individual's profile.

- Research Guidance: The software offers suggestions and guidance based on the information already input, helping users identify potential sources or records to search next.

- Multimedia: Users can attach photos, videos, sound clips, and other multimedia files to individuals and families in their tree.

- Geo Location Database: This feature assists users in finding places and standardizing place names, offering mapping and location tools to visualize ancestral homes and migration paths.

- Event Timelines: Users can see the historical and family events that occurred during an ancestor's life, helping place their ancestors in historical context.

- To-Do Lists and Research Logs: Legacy provides tools for users to organize their research tasks, note repositories to visit, records to look for, and more.

- DNA Tools: The software includes features to help users manage and analyze DNA test results, a growing area of interest in genealogy.

- Webinars: Legacy Family Tree offers a series of webinars on various topics in genealogy, providing education and guidance to both beginners and advanced researchers.

- Compatibility and Integration: While Legacy is a standalone program, it allows for integration with online databases and platforms, such as FamilySearch, to assist with research and tree syncing.

Editions and Pricing

- Standard Edition: Legacy Family Tree offers a free Standard edition with basic functionalities suitable for those new to genealogy software.

- Deluxe Edition: This is the paid version of the software, which unlocks a range of advanced features and tools not available in the Standard edition.

Legacy Family Tree is a popular and robust genealogy software choice for individuals interested in documenting and presenting their family history. It combines traditional genealogical research tools with modern features, such as DNA analysis tools, to cater to the diverse needs of family history researchers.

WikiTree

WikiTree is a collaborative, community-based genealogy website that allows users to create, share, and research family trees with the goal of creating a single, worldwide family tree. Its unique approach to genealogy research emphasizes accuracy, sourcing, and privacy, making it a valuable resource for both amateur and professional genealogists. Here's how WikiTree can be utilized for genealogy research:

Collaborative Family Trees

- One Profile per Ancestor: WikiTree's model ensures that each person has only one profile, which members can collaboratively edit and update. This helps in avoiding duplication and promotes the sharing of accurate, sourced information.

- Connection to the Global Tree: By contributing to WikiTree, you're not just building your own family tree; you're connecting your research to the larger, global tree, potentially discovering distant relatives and ancestors shared with other users

Sourcing and Reliability

- Emphasis on Sources: WikiTree encourages the citation of sources for all information, which enhances the reliability of the data. Users are prompted to include sources for birth dates, marriage details, death information, and other vital information, ensuring that the family tree is backed by evidence.

- Collaborative Research: The community aspect of WikiTree means that other researchers can contribute information, corrections, and sources to profiles, improving the overall quality and accuracy of the genealogical data.

Privacy Controls

- Privacy Settings: WikiTree provides robust privacy controls that allow you to protect sensitive information about living relatives. There are multiple privacy levels, from completely public for deceased ancestors to private settings for living people, ensuring compliance with privacy laws and ethical standards.

Tools and Features

- DNA Features: WikiTree integrates DNA test results to help in confirming family relationships. By connecting your DNA test results to your family tree, you can collaborate with others to find common ancestors and verify connections.

- Relationship Finder: This tool allows you to discover how you are related to other users and historical figures within the WikiTree database, offering interesting insights into your family's connections.

Community and Support

- G2G Forum: The Genealogist-to-Genealogist (G2G) Forum is a place where members can ask questions, seek help, and share news. It's a supportive environment where both beginners and experts can learn from each other.

- Projects and Challenges: WikiTree hosts a variety of themed projects and challenges that focus on specific ancestries, geographical areas, or historical periods. These projects offer opportunities for focused collaboration and research.

- Mentorship and Help: New users can benefit from WikiTree's mentorship program, which pairs novices with experienced genealogists to help navigate the site and improve research skills.

How to Use WikiTree for Your Research

- Create a Free Account: Start by signing up for a free account, which allows you to build your family tree and connect with other researchers.

- Enter Your Ancestors: Begin with what you know, entering details about your immediate family and ancestors, and then gradually work your way back. Remember to cite sources for the information you add.

- Connect with Relatives: As you add information, WikiTree will alert you to potential matches with existing profiles, helping you connect with distant relatives and integrate your research into the global tree.

- Participate in the Community: Engage with the WikiTree community through forums, projects, and challenges to get the most out of your genealogy research.

WikiTree's model of a free, collaborative platform makes it a unique and powerful tool for genealogy research. Its emphasis on accuracy, privacy, and community collaboration offers a comprehensive approach to building and verifying your family history within the context of a global family tree.

Find A Grave

Find A Grave is a website that allows users to search, add, and share cemetery records and tombstone inscriptions, is an invaluable resource for genealogy research. Owned by Ancestry.com, it hosts a vast database of cemetery records from around the world, making it one of the largest collections of burial information on the internet. Here's how you can use Find A Grave for genealogy research:

Searching for Ancestors

- Database Search: You can search for ancestors by entering their names, birth and death years, and locations into the search tool. This can return results from millions of cemetery records, including photos of tombstones, burial information, and other details provided by contributors.

- Location Browsing: If you have a general idea of where an ancestor was buried but not specific details, you can browse by cemetery location. This can be particularly useful for finding relatives buried in the same or nearby cemeteries.

Tombstone and Cemetery Records

- Tombstone Inscriptions: Tombstones often provide vital information, such as birth and death dates, and sometimes additional details like family relationships, epitaphs, and symbols that can give insights into the deceased's life or occupation. Tombstones are useful but NOT considered a primary source or vital record.

- Cemetery Information: Find A Grave includes information on cemeteries themselves, which can be helpful for understanding regional burial practices or planning visits to ancestors' gravesites.

Memorials
- Creating Memorials: Users can create online memorials for deceased relatives, including those not yet documented on the site. These memorials can include photographs of the person, tombstone, cemetery, and other relevant images, as well as biographical information and tributes.

- Contributing Information: If you find a memorial for an ancestor, you can contribute additional information or corrections, submit photo requests, or leave virtual flowers and notes as a way to honor and remember your ancestors.

Connecting with Other Researchers
- Message Boards and Requests: Find A Grave includes features for requesting photos of tombstones and connecting with other users who might have additional information about your ancestors or who are researching the same family lines or cemeteries.

Research Benefits
- Primary Source Material: Tombstone information serves as a primary source, which can be crucial for verifying birth and death dates, spelling of names, and family relationships.

- Discovering Unknown Relatives: Browsing cemetery records can lead to the discovery of previously unknown relatives buried in proximity to known ancestors.

Tips for Using Find A Grave Effectively
- Check Alternate Spellings: Names may be recorded differently over time or by mistake. Try various spellings if your initial search doesn't yield results.

- Explore Nearby Graves: Relatives are often buried near each other. Exploring memorials in the same cemetery can uncover additional family members.

- Use Advanced Search Options: Narrow your search with additional details you know about your ancestor to improve accuracy, especially in common names.

- Contribute: By adding memorials, photos, and accurate information, you help grow the resource for everyone and might even connect with distant relatives researching the same ancestors.

Find A Grave is a powerful tool for genealogists, providing access to a wealth of burial information that can fill in gaps in family history research, confirm dates and relationships, and offer new avenues for discovering ancestors.

Military Records

The best sources for military records, particularly in the United States, vary depending on the time period and branch of service. However, some key resources are widely recognized for their comprehensive collections and accessibility. These include:

- National Archives and Records Administration (NARA): NARA is perhaps the most important source for U.S. military records. It holds federal military service records from the Revolutionary War to the present, including personnel files, muster rolls, pension records, and more. The records can be accessed through their website or by visiting one of their physical locations.

- Fold3: This is a subscription-based website that specializes in military records, including service records, pension records, and military histories. It is particularly useful for digitized records and has a partnership with NARA to provide access to a wide range of documents.

- Ancestry.com: Another subscription-based service, Ancestry.com, has a substantial collection of military records. While it covers a range of genealogical records, its military collection includes draft registrations, service records, pension records, and more, from various conflicts.

- FamilySearch: Operated by The Church of Jesus Christ of Latter-day Saints, FamilySearch is a free online service that offers access to a variety of records, including military records. While its military collection is not as extensive as some paid services, it's a valuable resource, especially for those starting their research.

- U.S. Department of Veterans Affairs: For more recent military service records, the National Cemetery Administration (part of the VA) maintains records of veterans buried in national cemeteries. They also provide resources for obtaining service records.

- Library of Congress: The Library of Congress has various collections that include military records, particularly for historical research. This includes photographs, documents, and other archival material.

- State Archives and Military Museums: Many states have archives and military museums that hold records related to units raised within the state or residents who served in the military.

- The American Battle Monuments Commission: For those researching individuals who died in overseas military service, particularly in World Wars I and II, this commission maintains databases of those interred or memorialized at American military cemeteries and memorials abroad.

- Military Service Branch Archives: Each branch of the U.S. military has its own archive for historical records, such as the Army Heritage and Education Center, the Naval History and Heritage Command, and the National Museum of the Air Force.

It's important to note that access to some military records may be restricted, especially for records of service members who served more recently, due to privacy laws and regulations. Additionally, researchers often need to know specific details about the service member (such as full name, service number, and branch of service) to effectively locate records.

American Revolutionary War Records

For researching American Revolutionary War records, there are several key sources that provide extensive collections and valuable information. These resources are crucial for genealogists, historians, and anyone interested in the Revolutionary period:

- National Archives and Records Administration (NARA): NARA is the primary federal repository for Revolutionary War records. It holds military service records, pension and bounty land warrant applications, and other related documents. These records can be accessed through their online catalog or by visiting NARA facilities.

- Fold3: This is a subscription-based website specializing in military records. Fold3 has a substantial collection of Revolutionary War records, including service records, pension files, and more, digitized in partnership with NARA.

- Ancestry.com: Another major genealogy website, Ancestry.com offers access to a range of Revolutionary War records. This includes compiled service records, pension applications, and rosters, among others. Access requires a subscription.

- Daughters of the American Revolution (DAR): The DAR has an extensive library and database that includes Revolutionary War service records and lineage information submitted by its members. Their Genealogical Research System (GRS) is available online and can be a valuable tool for identifying ancestors who participated in the war.

- Sons of the American Revolution (SAR): Similar to the DAR, the SAR maintains records and databases related to Revolutionary War ancestors. Their library contains unique collections that may aid in research.

- State Archives and Libraries: Many state archives and libraries have collections of Revolutionary War records, particularly for units and soldiers from that state. This can include muster rolls, letters, diaries, and other documents.

- Library of Congress: Their collections include a vast array of materials related to the Revolutionary War, including maps, manuscripts, and newspapers. The Library of Congress also provides online access to many of these collections.

- American Revolutionary War Soldiers & Sailors Database: Managed by the National Park Service, this database includes information on soldiers and sailors who served in the Revolutionary War.

- HeritageQuest Online: Often accessible for free through public libraries, HeritageQuest includes Revolutionary War pension and bounty land warrant application files.

- JSTOR and Other Academic Databases: For more scholarly research, academic databases like JSTOR can provide access to historical papers and publications related to the Revolutionary War.

Each of these sources offers different types of information, and researchers often need to consult multiple sources to obtain a comprehensive view of an ancestor's role and experiences during the Revolutionary War. Access to some records may require a subscription or a visit to a specific archive or library.

Civil War Records

For researching Civil War records in the United States, several key sources are renowned for their comprehensive collections and accessibility. These resources are invaluable for genealogists, historians, and anyone interested in Civil War history:

- National Archives and Records Administration (NARA): NARA is the primary repository for federal Civil War records. It holds service records, pension files, and unit histories for both Union and Confederate soldiers. These records can be accessed online through the National Archives Catalog and in person at NARA facilities.

- Fold3: This subscription-based website specializes in military records and has an extensive collection of Civil War records, including compiled service records, pension applications, and other documents. Fold3 has partnered with NARA and other institutions to digitize and make these records available online.

- Ancestry.com: Another major subscription-based genealogy website, Ancestry.com offers a wide range of Civil War records, including draft registration records, service records, pension records, and cemetery listings. They also provide access to the U.S. Federal Census records, which can be helpful for identifying individuals and families around the time of the Civil War.

- FamilySearch: A free online service provided by The Church of Jesus Christ of Latter-day Saints, FamilySearch has a collection of Civil War records, including service records and pension index cards. The availability of records can vary, but it's a valuable starting point for anyone beginning Civil War research.

- Civil War Soldiers and Sailors System (CWSS): Managed by the National Park Service, the CWSS database contains basic facts about servicemen who served on both sides during the Civil War, including their regiment, company, and rank.

- State Archives and Libraries: Many states maintain archives and libraries with collections of Civil War records, particularly for units and soldiers that originated from that state. These can include muster rolls, letters, diaries, and other documents.

- Library of Congress: Their collections include photographs, maps, manuscripts, and other documents related to the Civil War. The Library of Congress also has online collections that are easily accessible.

- American Battlefield Trust: While primarily focused on battlefield preservation, their website provides educational resources and articles related to the Civil War, which can be helpful for contextual understanding.

- Local Historical Societies and Museums: Local historical societies and museums often have unique collections of Civil War records, particularly for local units or residents who participated in the war.

These resources collectively offer a wealth of information for anyone researching Civil War ancestors or seeking a deeper understanding of the conflict and its participants. Remember, accessing some records may require a subscription or a visit to a physical archive or library.

Church Records

Church records can be invaluable for genealogical research, especially in cases where civil records are limited or non-existent. These records, typically created by religious institutions, can include baptisms, marriages, burials, membership lists, and more. Here are some of the best sources for accessing church records:

- FamilySearch: Operated by The Church of Jesus Christ of Latter-day Saints, FamilySearch is a free online service that offers a vast collection of church records from around the world. They have digitized records from many denominations and make them available through their online database.

- Ancestry.com: This subscription-based service has a substantial collection of church records. While it covers a wide range of genealogical records, its church record collection includes various denominations and is particularly strong for the United States, Canada, and Europe.

- Local Church Archives: Many churches maintain their own historical archives. For more recent records or specific denominations, contacting the church directly or visiting their archives (if available) can be the best approach.

- National and State Archives: Some church records have been deposited in national or state archives. These institutions often hold older records that have been transferred for preservation.

- Public Libraries and Local Historical Societies: Local libraries and historical societies frequently have collections of church records, especially for local congregations. They might also have microfilm or digital copies of original records.

- Online Archive Catalogs: Websites like ArchiveGrid can help locate church records in various archives and libraries. These platforms aggregate records from multiple sources, providing a broad search capability.

- The Church of England Records: For those researching English ancestry, the Church of England parish registers are a key resource. These records can be accessed through websites like TheGenealogist or Findmypast.

- Genealogical Societies: Some genealogical societies have specialized collections or databases for church records, particularly for specific ethnic groups or regions.

- Specialized Websites for Specific Denominations: Some denominations have dedicated websites or databases for their records. For example, JewishGen for Jewish records, Catholic Parish Registers at the NLI for Irish Catholic records, and German church records through websites like Archion.de.

- Cyndi's List: This is a comprehensive, categorized list of genealogy sites online. It includes a section dedicated to religious records, which can be an excellent starting point for finding church records.

It's important to note that access to church records can vary widely depending on the church's policy, the age of the records, and privacy considerations. In some cases, you may need to visit an archive, church, or library in person to access these records.

Wikipedia

Using Wikipedia for genealogy research can be an effective way to gather background information, understand historical contexts, and find leads to primary sources. While Wikipedia itself is not a primary source for genealogical data, it offers a wealth of knowledge that can aid in family history research. Here's how you can utilize Wikipedia in your genealogy work:

Historical Context and Background Information

- Place Histories: Wikipedia articles on towns, cities, regions, and countries can provide historical context about the places where your ancestors lived. Understanding the history of these areas, including migrations, wars, economic conditions, and boundary changes, can offer insights into your ancestors' lives and movements.

- Occupations and Social Status: Articles on historical occupations, social classes, and conditions can give you a better understanding of an ancestor's lifestyle, challenges, and societal status.

- Historical Events: Learning about events that occurred during your ancestors' lifetimes can provide context for their decisions, movements, and experiences. Wikipedia's extensive coverage of wars, natural disasters, social movements, and political changes can be particularly useful.

Finding Leads to Primary and Secondary Sources

- References and Bibliographies: Wikipedia articles often include citations and bibliographies that can lead you to primary and secondary sources. These references can direct you to books, academic papers, archives, and other resources specific to your research interests.

- External Links: Many Wikipedia pages include external links to websites, archives, and other resources. These can be particularly valuable for genealogical research, offering direct access to databases, historical societies, and digital libraries.

Genealogical and Biographical Information

- Notable Individuals: Wikipedia contains biographies of many notable individuals, including information on their origins, families, and descendants. While your ancestors may not have their own Wikipedia pages, they may be mentioned in the context of local history or connected to notable figures.

- Family Trees of Prominent Families: Some Wikipedia articles include family trees or information on the genealogy of prominent families, especially in articles about royalty, nobility, or historical figures. These can provide clues or context for your own research, especially if you suspect a connection to these families.

Using Wikipedia Wisely in Genealogy Research

- Verification: Always verify information found on Wikipedia with primary sources. Wikipedia is a great starting point, but its open-editing nature means that information should be double-checked.

- Cautious Use: Be cautious when using Wikipedia for information on less notable individuals or families. Information may be less reliable, not well-sourced, or subject to recent changes.

- Contribute: If you have well-sourced, verifiable information about your ancestors and it is relevant to a broader historical context, consider contributing to Wikipedia. This can help others in their research and ensure the accuracy and completeness of historical and genealogical information on the platform.

In summary, while Wikipedia should not be the endpoint of genealogical research, it serves as an excellent tool for gaining historical insights, understanding the broader context of ancestors' lives, and identifying resources for further investigation. By using Wikipedia judiciously and always corroborating its information with primary sources, genealogists can enrich their understanding and exploration of their family history.

Journal Storage (JSTOR)

JSTOR (short for Journal Storage) is a digital library and online research platform that provides access to thousands of academic journals, books, and primary sources in various fields of study. Established in 1995, JSTOR was originally conceived as a solution to the increasing costs and storage issues associated with maintaining large archives of academic journal back issues in libraries. Over time, it has evolved into a widely used resource for researchers, scholars, and students. Key aspects of JSTOR include:

- Content Coverage: JSTOR covers a wide range of disciplines, including arts and humanities, social sciences, science and technology, and more. It is particularly well-known for its collection of historical and scholarly journals.

- Archival Journals: One of the primary features of JSTOR is its archival collection of academic journals. It includes complete back runs of journals from the first volume to issues from a few years ago, providing a historical perspective on various topics.

- Recent Publications: While JSTOR is known for its archival collections, it also includes recent publications and current issues of various journals through its Current Scholarship Program.
- Books and Primary Sources: In addition to journals, JSTOR offers access to a growing collection of academic books and primary sources relevant to a wide array of research areas.
- Access and Subscription: Access to JSTOR is typically provided through educational institutions, libraries, and other organizations. Individuals can also access JSTOR through a personal subscription, and the platform offers free access to a limited number of articles for individuals who register.
- Research Tools: JSTOR provides various tools to facilitate research, including advanced search options, citation tools, and the ability to save searches and content for later reference.
- JSTOR for Teaching and Learning: The platform is widely used in academic settings for teaching and learning purposes. It provides students and educators with access to high-quality, peer-reviewed content.

JSTOR is a valuable resource for conducting scholarly research, offering a comprehensive and reliable repository of academic literature that is easily accessible online.

Search Engines

Using search engines like Chrome, Bing, DuckDuckGo, and Safari can significantly enhance your genealogy research by helping you locate a wide range of online resources. Here are some effective strategies for conducting genealogy searches with search engines:
- Specific and Detailed Queries: Start with specific details in your search queries. Include full names (with middle names or initials if known), dates, locations, and any other relevant details like occupations or affiliations. For example, "Robert J. Smith 1892 birth record Erie Pennsylvania" is more specific than just "Robert Smith birth record."
- Use Quotation Marks for Exact Matches: To search for an exact

phrase, such as a full name, place it in quotation marks. For example, "Mary Elizabeth Johnson" will yield more precise results than searching for the words without quotation marks.

- Utilize Boolean Operators: Boolean operators like AND, OR, and NOT (or the minus symbol -) can refine your search. For example, "John Anderson" AND "Civil War" OR "military service" NOT "World War."

- Incorporate Variations and Misspellings: Remember that names and places might have been spelled differently in historical records. Try different variations and common misspellings in your searches.

- Use Wildcards: Some search engines allow the use of wildcards for unknown or variable parts of a name. For example, searching for "Johnsn" will return results for both "Johnson" and "Johnston."

- Search Specific Types of Records: Specify the type of record you're looking for in your search, such as census records, military records, marriage records, etc., to narrow down the results.

- Leverage Site-Specific Searches: Use search engines to explore specific websites or domains. For instance, searching "site: findagrave.com John Anderson" will limit the search to the Find A Grave website.

- Explore Images and Newspapers: Use the image search feature to find photographs, historical documents, or maps. Many search engines also have dedicated sections for searching news, which can be useful for finding obituaries and other articles.

- Combine Online and Offline Research: While search engines are powerful tools, not all genealogical data is digitized and online. Use your online findings as a starting point and verify them with physical records from archives, libraries, and other sources.

- Stay Organized: Keep track of your search queries and results. This will help you avoid repeating searches and allow you to refine your strategies as needed.

- Check Multiple Search Engines: Different search engines may yield different results, so it's worth trying your searches on more than one platform.

- Look for Genealogy Forums and Groups: Sometimes, your best leads can come from online forums, message boards, or social media groups dedicated to genealogy where you can find tips, ask questions, and share information with other researchers.

Remember, patience and persistence are key in genealogy research. Not every search will yield immediate results, and the process often involves a lot of trial and error. Keep refining your searches based on the information you uncover, and be open to exploring different avenues and resources.

Chrome

Using Google's Chrome to search for genealogy records can be a highly effective strategy, as Google's powerful search capabilities can help uncover a wide array of resources. Here are some tips on how to use Google effectively for genealogy research:

- Use Specific Keywords: Be as specific as possible with your search queries. Include names, dates, locations, and other relevant details about your ancestors. For instance, instead of just searching for "John Smith," try "John Smith 1850 Census Philadelphia" or "John Smith Civil War Service Records."

- Quotation Marks for Exact Phrases: Use quotation marks to search for exact phrases. This is particularly useful for searching specific names or terms. For example, searching "John A. Smith" will yield results for that exact name, rather than pages that include John and Smith separately.

- Use the Minus Sign to Exclude Terms: If you're getting results that are irrelevant, use the minus sign to exclude certain words from your search. For example, if searching for "John Smith" brings up results for a famous author you're not interested in, try "John Smith -author."

- Search for Site-Specific Information: Use Google to search within a specific website by using the "site:" operator. For example, "site: ancestry.com John Smith" will return results only from Ancestry.com.

- Explore Google Books and Newspapers: Google Books and Google News Archive can be treasure troves for genealogists, offering access to a vast range of books and historical newspapers that might contain mentions of ancestors.

- Use Google Images: Sometimes a picture is worth a thousand words, especially in genealogy. Use Google Images to find photos, historical maps, and documents.

- Leverage Google Scholar: For more scholarly or historical information, use Google Scholar. It can help locate academic papers, theses, and publications that might reference an ancestor or the historical context they lived in.

- Utilize Google Alerts: Set up Google Alerts for your ancestors' names or specific search terms. This way, you'll be notified when new information matching your criteria appears online.

- Check Google Patents: If your ancestor was an inventor or involved in patent work, searching Google Patents could yield interesting results.

- Language Translation: If dealing with records in foreign languages, Google Translate can be a helpful tool.

Remember, while Google is a powerful tool for locating online genealogy resources, not all genealogical data is available online. You may need to complement your Google research with visits to archives, libraries, or other repositories. Additionally, always verify the information you find online with primary sources or reliable genealogy databases.

Bing

Conducting genealogy searches using Bing, Microsoft's search engine, can be an effective way to uncover a range of online resources relevant to your family history research. Here are some strategies and tips to optimize your genealogy searches on Bing:

- Specific and Detailed Search Queries: Start with detailed search queries. Include as much information as you have, such as full names (including middle names or initials), dates, locations, and any other pertinent details like occupations or affiliations.

- Quotation Marks for Exact Phrases: Use quotation marks to search for exact phrases. For instance, searching for "John A. Smith" in quotation marks will yield results for that exact name combination.

- Advanced Search Operators: Utilize Bing's advanced search operators like AND, OR, and NOT to refine your results. For example, "Margaret Johnson" AND "marriage record" NOT "obituary" will help filter the results more precisely.

- Search for Variants and Common Misspellings: Historical records often contain variations in spelling. Try different spellings and phonetic variants of names in your searches.

- Use of Wildcards: Bing supports the asterisk () as a wildcard character, which can be helpful if you're unsure of the complete name or term. For example, a search for "Robson family history" can return results for "Robinson," "Robertson," etc.

- Site-Specific Searches: Use Bing to search within specific websites. For example, "site: ancestry.com William Johnson military records" will return results only from Ancestry.com.

- Search in Different Categories: Bing offers different search categories like Web, Images, Videos, and News. Utilizing these can help find photos, historical documents, or news articles related to your family history.

- Use Bing Maps for Geographical Context: Bing Maps can be a useful tool for understanding the geographical context of your ancestors' lives. You can look up old addresses, explore historical maps, or view modern images of locations where your ancestors lived.

- Check Bing News for Recent Mentions: If you are looking for more recent family history or obituaries, Bing News can be a valuable resource.

- Stay Organized: Keep track of your search queries and results. This not only helps in avoiding repetition but also in refining your search strategies over time.

- Explore Bing Visual Search: For identifying places, buildings, or artifacts in family photographs, Bing's Visual Search feature can be quite useful.

- Combine Online and Offline Resources: Remember that not all genealogical information is available online. Use the findings from Bing as a starting point and corroborate them with physical records from libraries, archives, or other repositories.

Using Bing for genealogy research is similar to using other search engines but might yield different results or perspectives. It's beneficial to use it in conjunction with other resources and tools for a more comprehensive search strategy.

Duck Duck Go

Using DuckDuckGo for genealogy searches can be an effective approach, especially for those who prefer a search engine that prioritizes user privacy. DuckDuckGo doesn't track your searches or create a personal search history, which can be appealing to many users. Here are some strategies to make the most of your genealogy searches using DuckDuckGo:

•Detailed Search Queries: Start with specific and detailed queries. Include full names, dates, locations, and other relevant details. For instance, instead of just searching "John Smith," try "John Smith 1845 birth record Ohio" or "John Smith Civil War military records."

- Use Quotation Marks for Exact Phrases: To find exact matches, place names or specific phrases in quotation marks. For example, "Mary Elizabeth Johnson" will yield more precise results than searching for the words without quotation marks.

- Boolean Operators: DuckDuckGo supports Boolean operators like AND, OR, and a minus (-) sign for NOT. These can help refine your search. For example, "William Brown" AND "Revolutionary War" -basketball.

- Wildcard Searches: Like many other search engines, Duck-

DuckGo allows the use of asterisks (*) as wildcard characters to replace unknown or variable parts of a name or term.

- Search Variations and Common Misspellings: Historical records often contain different spellings of names. Try various spellings or phonetic equivalents in your searches.

- Location-Specific Searches: Include specific locations in your searches to narrow down results. For example, "Smith family cemetery records Kentucky".

- Search Specific Types of Records: Direct your search towards specific types of records by including terms like "census records", "military service", "land deeds", or "marriage records" in your query.

- Combine Online and Offline Research: Remember that Duck-DuckGo, like any other search engine, is just a starting point. Verify the information you find with primary sources or records from archives, libraries, or genealogical societies.

- Use DuckDuckGo Instant Answers for Quick Facts: For general historical facts or quick information, DuckDuckGo's Instant Answers can be useful.

- Search International Resources: If your research involves non-U.S. ancestors, include the country or region in your search terms to find relevant international resources.

- Stay Organized: Keep track of your search queries and results, especially since DuckDuckGo doesn't store your search history. This will help you avoid repeating the same searches and allow you to refine your strategies.

- Explore Related Topics: Use DuckDuckGo to find related topics or historical contexts that might give you new insights or directions in your research.

Using DuckDuckGo for genealogy requires creativity and persistence, much like any other search engine. While it doesn't offer personalized search results based on past searches, its straightforward search approach can sometimes bring up unique results not biased by previous search history.

Safari

Using Apple Safari, the web browser developed by Apple Inc., for genealogy research is a straightforward and efficient process, much like using any other web browser for research purposes. Safari is known for its clean interface, fast browsing speeds, and user-friendly features, making it a good choice for genealogists looking to explore their family history online. Here's how you can use Safari for genealogy research:

Accessing Online Databases and Archives

- Genealogy Websites: Safari provides access to a wide range of genealogy websites and databases, such as Ancestry.com, FamilySearch.org, Findmypast, and MyHeritage, where you can search for historical records, family trees, and other genealogical information. Simply type the URL of the website into the Safari address bar or use a search engine to find the site.

- Digital Libraries and Archives: Use Safari to visit digital libraries and archives, like the Digital Public Library of America (DPLA), Internet Archive, or the National Archives, to access digitized records, books, and documents relevant to your research.

Bookmarking and Organizing Resources

- Bookmarks: Safari allows you to bookmark important genealogy websites, databases, and specific pages you find useful, making it easier to return to them later. You can organize your bookmarks into folders, such as by surname or geographic location, for efficient access.

- Reading List: For articles or web pages you want to read later, Safari's Reading List feature is a convenient option. It saves pages for offline reading, which is particularly handy if you're researching without immediate internet access.

Using Tabs for Comparative Research

- Multiple Tabs: Safari supports opening multiple tabs simultaneously, enabling you to compare information from different sources side-by-side. This is useful when cross-referencing data from various genealogy records or when looking at multiple family trees.

Privacy and Security

- Private Browsing: When researching sensitive or personal family information, you might prefer to use Safari's Private Browsing mode, which doesn't save your browsing history, cookies, or site data.

- Security Features: Safari includes several security features, such as warning you about suspicious websites, which helps protect your personal information while conducting genealogy research online.

Extensions and Plugins

- Genealogy Extensions: Although Safari's selection of extensions is more limited compared to browsers like Chrome or Firefox, you can still find tools and plugins designed to enhance your genealogy research. These might include citation managers, note-taking apps, or tools that highlight names and dates on web pages.

Syncing Across Devices

- iCloud Integration: If you use multiple Apple devices, Safari's integration with iCloud can be particularly beneficial. You can sync bookmarks, Reading List items, and even open tabs across your Mac, iPhone, and iPad, allowing for seamless research across devices.

Screenshot and Markup Tools

- Capture Information: Safari's screenshot feature, coupled with Markup tools on macOS and iOS, allows you to capture and annotate web pages, records, and documents. This can be helpful for saving information and making notes for your genealogy files.

Using Safari for genealogy research offers a blend of convenience, speed, and features conducive to extensive online research. Its integration with other Apple services and devices further enhances the research experience, making it a solid choice for genealogists who prefer Apple's ecosystem.

Newspaper.com

Newspapers.com is a valuable resource for genealogy research, offering a vast collection of digitalized newspapers from various places and time periods. These newspapers can provide unique insights into your ancestors' lives, offering information not typically found in traditional genealogical records. Here's how to conduct effective genealogy searches on Newspapers.com:

- Basic Search: Start with a basic search using your ancestor's name. It's often effective to begin broadly and then narrow down your search based on the results you find.

- Advanced Search Options: Utilize the advanced search feature to refine your search. You can include specific keywords, dates, or newspaper titles. This is particularly useful for common names where you need to narrow down results.

- Use Quotation Marks for Exact Matches: When searching for a specific name or phrase, use quotation marks. This tells the search engine to look for the exact words in that specific order.

- Include Variations and Misspellings: Names and spellings can vary widely in historical newspapers. Try different variations of your ancestor's name and consider common misspellings or abbreviations.

- Search by Location: Focus your search on newspapers from locations where your ancestor lived. Local newspapers often have detailed stories about residents, including obituaries, marriage announcements, social activities, and legal notices.

- Check Different Time Periods: Extend your search beyond your ancestor's lifespan. Newspapers might contain references to them posthumously, in family histories, or in the context of their descendants' news stories.

- Obituaries and Marriage Announcements: These are particularly rich sources of information in newspapers. Obituaries can provide names of family members, birth and death dates, and other personal details, while marriage announcements can include similar valuable information.

- Read Entire Articles for Context: Sometimes, the most valuable information isn't in a headline but hidden within the article. Reading entire articles can provide context and additional details.

- Save and Organize Your Findings: When you find relevant articles, save them. Newspapers.com allows you to clip articles and save them to your account, which can be organized into folders.

- Cite Your Sources: Keep track of where and when you found each piece of information for future reference, especially if you plan to share your genealogical research.

- Explore Community Contributions: Check clippings made by other users. Sometimes, other researchers may have already clipped articles about your ancestors or their associates.

Remember, access to Newspapers.com usually requires a subscription, although they sometimes offer free access weekends or trials. Additionally, not all newspapers are available on this platform, so it may be necessary to supplement your research with other newspaper archives or resources.

Mormon Church

The Church of Jesus Christ of Latter-day Saints, commonly referred to as the Mormon Church, has extensive resources for conducting genealogical research. They offer both physical and digital resources that are widely recognized for their depth and usefulness, even for those who are not members of the church. Here's how to use these resources:

FamilySearch Website:

- The church operates FamilySearch (familysearch.org), one of the largest free genealogy websites in the world. You can start here by creating a free account.

- Once you have an account, you can search through billions of historical records, including birth, marriage, death, census, military, and church records from all over the world.

- FamilySearch also allows you to build and maintain your family tree online, offering tools to connect with other researchers who might be related to you or researching similar family lines.

Family History Centers:

- The church operates over 4,600 Family History Centers worldwide. These are branch facilities of the Family History Library in Salt Lake City, Utah, and they provide access to genealogical records and personal assistance from knowledgeable volunteers.
- At these centers, you can access specialized genealogical software and databases, some of which might require payment if accessed from home. Use of these resources at the centers is free.
- To find a Family History Center near you, use the FamilySearch website's location tool.

Family History Library:

- The main library in Salt Lake City houses an extensive collection of genealogical records. If you can visit, you'll have access to millions of microfilms, books, and digital resources from around the globe, along with assistance from expert genealogists.
- For those who cannot visit in person, many of the library's resources are digitized and available through the FamilySearch website, and they continue to digitize more records regularly.

Consultation and Classes:

- Both online and at local centers, the church offers free classes and personal consultation services to help you get started with genealogy or to overcome research obstacles. These resources are invaluable for both beginners and experienced researchers.
- Check the FamilySearch website for webinars, video tutorials, and information on how to get help with your research.
- Collaborative Research Tools:
- FamilySearch encourages collaboration among researchers. You can connect with others who may be researching the same family lines, share information, and work together to build a more complete family history.

Respect Privacy:

When using FamilySearch or any other genealogical tool, be mindful of privacy concerns, especially when dealing with information about living individuals.

The Church of Jesus Christ of Latter-day Saints provides these resources as part of its commitment to family history and genealogical research. Their resources are open to everyone, regardless of religious affiliation, and they are an excellent starting point for anyone interested in tracing their ancestry.

Genealogy Organizations

Difference between a Historical and Genealogical Society

Historical and genealogical societies both play crucial roles in preserving the past, but they focus on different aspects of history and serve slightly different purposes. Here's a breakdown of the primary differences between the two:

Historical Societies
Focus: Historical societies concentrate on collecting, preserving, and interpreting the history of a particular area, community, or theme. This includes a broad spectrum of interests such as social, cultural, political, and economic aspects of history.
Collections: Their collections often include a wide variety of items such as artifacts, photographs, documents, and maps that reflect the history of an area or subject matter. These items are preserved for their historical value and the insights they provide into the past.
Activities: Historical societies frequently engage in activities like maintaining museums or historic sites, organizing exhibitions, publishing historical research, and conducting educational programs and lectures for the public.
Audience: While they serve researchers and historians, they also aim to engage the general public's interest in history, offering insights into how the past shapes the present and future.
Genealogical Societies

Focus: Genealogical societies are dedicated to studying and tracing family ancestries and lineages. They focus on the personal histories of individuals and families, helping people connect with their ancestors and understand their family's place in history.
Collections: Their collections are rich in records useful for genealogical research, such as birth, marriage, death records, census data, immigration and emigration records, and other personal documents. These societies may also hold or have access to databases and software specialized for genealogical research.
Activities: Genealogical societies offer resources and guidance for conducting family history research, including workshops, seminars, and guidance on using genealogical tools and resources. They often provide assistance with DNA testing and interpretation, helping individuals to trace their lineage and find relatives.
Audience: Their primary audience consists of individuals researching their family history, from hobbyists to professional genealogists. They cater to anyone looking to uncover their ancestry, discover their family's story, and connect with distant relatives.
Key Differences
- Scope of Interest: Historical societies have a broader focus on the collective history of communities and societies, while genealogical societies zero in on individual and family histories.

- Type of Collections: Historical societies collect a wide range of historical artifacts and documents, whereas genealogical societies focus on records that can help trace familial relationships and lineages.

- Purpose and Activities: The main purpose of historical societies is to preserve and educate about the broader historical narrative, offering a wide range of public programs. Genealogical societies, on the other hand, focus on providing resources, tools, and education specifically for tracing family histories.

- Audience Engagement: Both societies engage with the public but cater to different interests: one towards a general historical interest and the other towards personal or familial history research.

In summary, while historical and genealogical societies both preserve important aspects of the past, they differ in focus, collections, activities, and the audiences they serve. Each plays a unique role in helping individuals and communities understand their place in the tapestry of history.

Major Genealogical Societies in USA

The United States is home to a wide array of genealogical societies, each serving different interests, regions, and aspects of genealogy. Some of the major genealogical societies in the USA include:

- National Genealogical Society (NGS): A premier national society for genealogists of all levels, providing education and resources.

- New England Historic Genealogical Society (NEHGS): America's oldest genealogical society, focusing on New England ancestry.

- Daughters of the American Revolution (DAR): For women who can trace their lineage to an ancestor who contributed to American independence.

- Sons of the American Revolution (SAR): Similar to DAR but for male descendants of those who contributed to American independence.

- The Mayflower Society (General Society of Mayflower Descendants): For descendants of the passengers of the Mayflower.

- African American Genealogical Society (AAGS): Focusing on African American genealogy.

- American-French Genealogical Society (AFGS): Dedicated to the study of French-Canadian genealogy.

- National Society, Sons of the Union Veterans of the Civil War: For male descendants of Union soldiers in the American Civil War.

- National Society of the Colonial Dames of America (NSCDA): A society for women who are descended from an ancestor who lived in an American colony.

- Federation of Genealogical Societies (FGS): A coalition of genealogical societies across the country, focusing on strengthening and supporting member organizations.

- Jewish Genealogical Society (JGS): Concentrating on Jewish genealogy.
- Hispanic Genealogical Society of New York: Focusing on Hispanic and Latino genealogy.
- Irish Genealogical Society International (IGSI): Specializing in Irish genealogy.
- Swedish American Genealogical Society: Focusing on Swedish genealogy.
- Germanic Genealogy Society (GGS): Dedicated to German genealogy.
- Polish Genealogical Society of America (PGSA): Specializing in Polish ancestry.
- Italian Genealogical Group (IGG): Focused on Italian genealogy.
- Chinese Family History Group of Southern California: Concentrating on Chinese genealogy.
- General Society of Colonial Wars: For male descendants of those who served in specific roles during the Colonial era.

These societies often provide resources such as libraries, archives, publications, seminars, and workshops to help individuals research their ancestry. They may also offer membership, which typically includes access to additional resources and participation in society events.

National Genealogy Society

The National Genealogical Society (NGS), founded in 1903, is a prominent organization in the United States dedicated to genealogy and family history. It is a non-profit organization with a mission to educate and support genealogists of all skill levels, from hobbyists to professionals. Here are key aspects of the National Genealogical Society:

- Education and Training: NGS provides a wide range of educational resources, including webinars, online courses, and an annual conference that features lectures, workshops, and seminars. These resources cover various aspects of genealogical research, methodology, and best practices.

- Publications: The society publishes several resources, including the "NGS Quarterly," a scholarly journal that presents genealogical case studies and methodological insights, and the "NGS Magazine," which offers articles on genealogical techniques and resources.

- Research Resources: NGS offers guidance and tools to assist members with their research. This includes special publications like research guides and reference books.

- Advocacy and Standards: The organization plays a role in promoting standards and ethics in genealogical research. It advocates for access to public records and works to promote high-quality research practices.

- Community and Networking: NGS provides opportunities for genealogists to connect, share, and collaborate through its conferences, local chapters, and online platforms.

- Special Interest Groups: The society caters to diverse interests within the field of genealogy, including specific geographic areas, ethnic research, and special topics.

- Membership Benefits: Members of the NGS receive access to exclusive content, discounts on publications and conference registrations, and other benefits.

- Outreach and Support for Genealogical Societies: NGS supports local genealogical societies with resources and guidelines for society management, programming, and outreach.

- Online Store: They offer an online store where members and non-members can purchase genealogical books, guides, and NGS merchandise.

- Collaboration with Other Organizations: NGS collaborates with other genealogical and historical organizations to advance the field of genealogy and to provide a broader range of resources

and services to its members.
The National Genealogical Society is recognized for its commitment to excellence in genealogy and for providing support and resources to the genealogical community in the United States and beyond. Its efforts are geared towards both preserving and advancing the field of genealogy for future generations.
Founded: 1903
Location: Falls Church, Virginia
Membership: over 10,000

GenTech Inc.
GenTech, a division of the National Genealogical Society (NGS), serves as a bridge between genealogy and technology. It is particularly known for the development of the GenTech Genealogical Data Model, which is a valuable resource for software developers who create genealogy software. This model provides a formal framework for understanding and organizing genealogical data and the genealogical research process, making it a significant contribution to the field, especially for those interested in the technological aspects of genealogy.
The National Genealogical Society, to which GenTech belongs, has a long history of leading in genealogy, having been established in 1903. NGS is noted for its contributions to genealogical education through conferences, seminars, workshops, and research tours. Additionally, it offers a variety of publications, including books, magazines, and the National Genealogical Society Quarterly. They also introduced the NGS Home Study Course in American Genealogy in 1981, which has evolved into offering online courses in American Genealogy and special subject matter courses developed by experts.

Daughters of the American Revolution (DAR)

The Daughters of the American Revolution (DAR) is a lineage-based membership organization for women who are directly descended from a person involved in the United States' efforts towards independence. Established in 1890, the DAR is dedicated to promoting historic preservation, education, and patriotism. Here are key aspects of the organization:

- Membership: To join the DAR, a woman must prove lineal descent from a patriot of the American Revolution. This can be an ancestor who fought in the war, provided aid, or contributed in other significant ways to the independence cause.

- Historic Preservation: One of the primary objectives of the DAR is to preserve historical artifacts, buildings, and sites associated with the American Revolution. The organization often restores and maintains historic properties and collects and preserves artifacts and documents from that period.

- Education: The DAR supports various educational programs and resources, including scholarships, contests for students, and support for schools. They aim to educate the public about the history of the American Revolution and the founding principles of the United States.

- Patriotism: The organization encourages patriotic activities and loyalty to the United States. This includes supporting veterans, promoting the Constitution, and participating in civic duties.

- Community Service: Members of the DAR engage in various forms of community service, from volunteering at veterans' hospitals to participating in literacy programs.

- National Headquarters: The DAR operates a national headquarters in Washington, D.C., which includes a museum, a library, and the organization's administrative offices.

- Historical Research and Genealogy: The DAR Library is one of the nation's premier genealogical research centers, and the organization places a strong emphasis on genealogical research, helping members and others trace their lineage to ancestors who contributed to the American Revolution.

The DAR has grown into a significant and influential organization, with chapters throughout the United States and in several other countries. Its members are committed to preserving the legacy of those who fought for or supported the cause of American independence.

Founders: Mary S. Lockwood, Eleen Harding Walworth, Eugenia

Washington, Mary Desha
Headquarters: Washington, D.C.
Founded: October 11, 1890
Member number: 190,000
Website: www.dar.org

Sons of the American Revolution (SAR)

The Sons of the American Revolution (SAR) is a lineage-based membership organization for men who are descendants of those who supported the independence of the United States during the American Revolutionary War. It shares similar objectives and principles with the Daughters of the American Revolution (DAR), but is a separate entity. Key aspects of the SAR include:

- Membership: Membership in the SAR is open to men who can demonstrate lineal descent from a person who rendered active service in the cause of American independence, whether as soldiers, seamen, civil officers, or other roles that contributed to the Revolutionary effort.

- Objectives and Missions: The SAR focuses on patriotic, historical, and educational activities. It aims to instill appreciation for the principles of governance established by the U.S. Constitution and the sacrifices of Revolutionary War ancestors.

- Historical Preservation: The organization is actively involved in preserving records, artifacts, and historical sites related to the American Revolution. This includes participating in or sponsoring restoration projects and historical research.

- Education and Scholarships: The SAR provides various educational resources and sponsors competitions and scholarships for students. They aim to promote knowledge about the events and principles of the American Revolution and the nation's founding.

- Patriotism and Civic Involvement: The SAR encourages patriotic observance, respect for national symbols like the flag, and participation in civic activities. Members often participate in parades, memorial services, and other patriotic events.

- Genealogical Research: Like the DAR, the SAR places significant emphasis on genealogical research. They assist members and others in tracing their lineage to Revolutionary War ancestors and encourage the study of family history.

- Community Service: Members of the SAR engage in various forms of community service and support for patriotic and historical education initiatives.

Established in 1889, the SAR operates chapters throughout the United States and has international societies in several countries. The organization works closely with other historical and patriotic groups to promote understanding and appreciation of the legacy of the American Revolution.

Founded: April 30, 1889

Founder: William Osborne McDowell

Affiliations: Daughters of the American Revolution, Children of the American Revolution

Headquarters: 809 West Main St., Louisville, Kentucky

National Society of the Children of the American Revolution (NSCAR)

The National Society of the Children of the American Revolution (N.S.C.A.R.) is a youth organization founded in 1895 for individuals under the age of 21 who are descendants of individuals who served or contributed to the cause of American independence during the Revolutionary War. It is the oldest patriotic youth organization in the United States and operates under the patronage of the Daughters of the American Revolution (DAR) and the Sons of the American Revolution (SAR). Key aspects of the Children of the American Revolution include:

- Membership: Membership is open to children and youth who can trace their lineage to someone who supported the American Revolution. This includes soldiers, sailors, civil officers, and others who contributed to the cause.

- Objectives: The organization aims to train good citizens, develop leaders, and promote love of the United States and its heritage among young people.

- Education and Patriotic Activities: The C.A.R. engages in various educational and patriotic activities, encouraging its members to learn about the history of the American Revolution and the foundational principles of the United States.

- Leadership Development: The organization offers opportunities for leadership at local, state, and national levels. Members can hold various positions and participate in decision-making processes, helping them develop leadership skills.

- Community Service: Members are involved in community service projects that promote awareness of American heritage, support veterans, and contribute to historic preservation.

- Meetings and Events: The C.A.R. holds meetings and events where members learn about American history, engage in civic activities, and participate in organizational governance.

- Connection to DAR and SAR: While independent, the C.A.R. maintains a close relationship with the DAR and SAR, often participating in joint activities and benefiting from the guidance and support of these related organizations.

The Children of the American Revolution offers a platform for young people to explore their American heritage, engage in patriotic activities, and develop as future leaders and responsible citizens.

Founded: April 5, 1895
Founder: Harriet Lothrop
Headquarters: Washington, DC
Website: www.nscar.org

Mayflower Society

The Mayflower Society, formally known as The General Society of Mayflower Descendants, is a hereditary organization for individuals who can trace their lineage back to passengers on the Mayflower, the ship that brought the first Pilgrim settlers to New

England in 1620. Founded in 1897, the society is dedicated to preserving the history and legacy of these Pilgrim ancestors. Key aspects of the Mayflower Society include:

- Membership: To become a member, an individual must provide documentation proving direct descent from one or more of the Mayflower passengers. The application process is rigorous and requires thorough genealogical research.

- Educational Activities: The society is involved in various educational initiatives aimed at promoting understanding of the Pilgrims' history and their significance in American history. This includes supporting research, publications, and educational programs related to Pilgrim history.

- Preservation of Heritage: The Mayflower Society works to preserve the cultural and historical heritage of the Pilgrims, including maintaining historical sites and artifacts associated with the Mayflower voyage and the early colonial period in New England.

- Commemoration and Celebration: The organization holds events and activities to commemorate significant dates related to the Mayflower and the Pilgrims, such as the anniversary of the Mayflower's landing at Plymouth Rock.

- Community and Scholarship Programs: The society often sponsors and participates in community service projects and scholarship programs that align with its mission of preserving Pilgrim history and promoting education.

- Library and Archives: The Mayflower Society operates a library and maintains archives that house a collection of books, manuscripts, and other materials related to the Pilgrims and early American history.

- Publications: The society publishes scholarly and educational materials, including a journal that features historical research, genealogical studies, and information about the society's activities.

The Mayflower Society plays a significant role in preserving the legacy of the Pilgrims and promoting an understanding of their contributions to American history. Its members are dedicated

to honoring the memory and achievements of their Mayflower ancestors.
Founded: 1897
Headquarters: Plymouth, MA
Membership: Over 31,000
Number: 35 million Mayflower

General Society of the Colonial Wars

The General Society of Colonial Wars is an organization in the United States for men who can trace their lineage to an ancestor who served in a military or civil position during the Colonial period of American history, specifically between the settlement of Jamestown in 1607 and the Battle of Lexington in 1775. Established in 1892, the society focuses on commemorating and preserving the history of this era. Key aspects of the General Society of Colonial Wars include:

- Membership: Membership is open to adult males who can prove lineal descent from an ancestor who played a role in the establishment, defense, or expansion of the American colonies. This includes ancestors who served in military, naval, or civil capacities during the specified period.

- Historical Preservation: The society is actively involved in preserving historical records, artifacts, and sites related to the Colonial period of American history. This includes supporting restoration projects, historical research, and educational initiatives.

- Education and Scholarship: The society promotes the study and understanding of Colonial American history through various means, including sponsoring scholarships, lectures, and publications.

- Patriotic Activities: The organization participates in and sponsors events that commemorate significant events and figures from the Colonial period. These activities often involve collaboration with other historical and patriotic societies.

- Community Engagement and Service: Members are encouraged to engage in community service and activities that promote an understanding of America's colonial heritage.

- Meetings and Gatherings: The society organizes meetings, dinners, and other events where members gather to discuss historical topics, conduct society business, and promote fellowship among members.

- State Societies: The General Society of Colonial Wars comprises various state societies, each with its own membership and activities but united under the umbrella of the national organization.

The General Society presently comprises some thirty-two constituent state societies. The organization was founded in New York in 1892, originally as a state society. The General Society was founded in 1893. Current members have been invited to join only after fulfilling their State Society's individual application procedures and membership requirements. It is in one or more of the State Societies that an individual holds membership, and the collective federation of State Societies constitutes the General Society.

The General Society of Colonial Wars plays a vital role in keeping alive the memory of the people and events of the Colonial era in American history, emphasizing the importance of this period in the formation of the United States. Its activities are aimed at educating the public and its members about the challenges, achievements, and legacy of the early American settlers and leaders.
Founded: 1892 -1893
Members: 4,000 - 4,500
Website: www.gscw.org

State Genealogical Societies

State Genealogical Society

A state genealogical society is an organization dedicated to preserving, collecting, and disseminating genealogical knowledge and resources within a specific state. These societies play a crucial role in helping individuals trace their family histories, understand their ancestry, and connect with others who have similar interests in genealogy. Here's a detailed overview of what a state genealogy society typically encompasses:

Mission and Objectives

- The primary mission is to promote an interest in genealogical research and preserve genealogical records, documents, and artifacts relevant to the state.

- Objectives often include providing educational resources, workshops, and seminars to help members and the public improve their genealogical research skills.

Activities and Services

- Research Assistance: Many societies maintain libraries or archives with collections of historical and genealogical records, including books, manuscripts, microfilms, and digital databases that are specific to the state's history and families.

- Publications: They frequently publish newsletters, journals, or magazines featuring articles on genealogical research methods, case studies, and discoveries related to the state's history.

- Workshops and Seminars: Educational events are common, aimed at both beginners and experienced researchers, covering topics from basic genealogy research techniques to the use of DNA in genealogy.

- Special Interest Groups: Some societies have groups focused on specific research interests, such as DNA genealogy, military ancestors, or specific ethnic groups.

- Online Resources: Many state genealogy societies offer a range of online resources, including searchable databases, digital archives, and forums for members to share information and collaborate on research.

Membership

- Membership is typically open to anyone with an interest in genealogy, whether they are beginners, experienced researchers, or professionals.

- Members may receive benefits such as access to exclusive resources, discounts on publications and events, and the opportunity to participate in special projects.

Community and Collaboration

- State genealogy societies often collaborate with libraries, archives, and other historical organizations to preserve and make accessible historical records.

- They may also engage in projects to digitize records, index documents, and create databases that are invaluable for genealogical research.

- Societies provide a community for those interested in genealogy to share their findings, exchange ideas, and support each other in their research endeavors.

Contribution to Genealogical Research

- By preserving and indexing historical records, state genealogy societies make significant contributions to the field of genealogy, enabling researchers to trace their ancestry and learn about the lives of their ancestors.

- They play a vital role in advocating for the preservation of historical records and cemeteries, ensuring that future generations have access to these important resources.

In summary, a state genealogy society is an indispensable resource for anyone interested in exploring their family history, offering access to specialized knowledge, resources, and a community of like-minded individuals. These societies not only assist individuals in their personal research but also contribute to the broader understanding and preservation of the state's genealogical heritage.

Below is a list of genealogical societies in each state of the United States. These societies focus on the genealogical research and history specific to their respective states, providing valuable resources, databases, publications, and support for individuals researching their family history within that state. Please note that some states may have more than one society, and there are also

numerous local and regional genealogy societies not listed here.
A List of State Genealogical Societies

- Alabama Genealogical Society

- Alaska Genealogical Society

- Arizona Genealogical Advisory Board (No specific statewide society, but multiple regional groups)

- Arkansas Genealogical Society

- California Genealogical Society and Library

- Colorado Genealogical Society

- Connecticut Society of Genealogists, Inc.

- Delaware Genealogical Society

- Florida State Genealogical Society

- Georgia Genealogical Society

- Hawaii Genealogical Society (Various societies for different islands/regions)

- Idaho Genealogical Society

- Illinois State Genealogical Society

- Indiana Genealogical Society

- Iowa Genealogical Society

- Kansas Genealogical Society

- Kentucky Genealogical Society

- Louisiana Genealogical & Historical Society

- Maine Genealogical Society

- Maryland Genealogical Society

- Massachusetts Society of Genealogists

- Michigan Genealogical Council

- Minnesota Genealogical Society

- Mississippi Genealogical Society

- Missouri State Genealogical Association

- Montana State Genealogical Society

- Nebraska Genealogical Society
- Nevada Genealogical Society (Note: Specific societies like the Clark County Nevada Genealogy Society may serve as the primary resource.)
- New Hampshire Society of Genealogists
- New Jersey Genealogical Society
- New Mexico Genealogical Society
- New York Genealogical and Biographical Society
- North Carolina Genealogical Society
- North Dakota State Genealogical Society
- Ohio Genealogical Society
- Oklahoma Genealogical Society
- Oregon Genealogical Society
- Pennsylvania Genealogical Society
- Rhode Island Genealogical Society
- South Carolina Genealogical Society
- South Dakota Genealogical Society
- Tennessee Genealogical Society
- Texas State Genealogical Society
- Utah Genealogical Association
- Vermont French-Canadian Genealogical Society (Vermont does not have a state-wide genealogical society but has specialized societies like this one.)
- Virginia Genealogical Society
- Washington State Genealogical Society
- West Virginia Genealogical Society
- Wisconsin State Genealogical Society
- Wyoming State Historical Society (Also serves as the state's genealogical society)

Please note that the existence and names of these societies may change over time, and there may be new societies formed or existing ones that may dissolve or merge. It's always a good idea to look up the most current information directly from the society's website or contact them for the most up-to-date resources and membership information.

State Genealogical Organizations (examples)

New York
An example of a state genealogical society is the "New York Genealogical and Biographical Society" (NYG&B). Established in 1869, the NYG&B is the oldest and one of the most prominent state genealogical societies in the United States, dedicated to assisting researchers of New York State family history and genealogy.
Mission and Objectives
- The NYG&B's mission is to help people of all backgrounds discover their family history and explore the unique history of New York State. It aims to educate, inspire, and connect researchers as they explore their family's past.

Resources and Collections

- Library Collections: The NYG&B maintains a vast collection of New York State genealogical and historical resources, including family genealogies, local histories, church records, and more.

- Digital Collections: The society offers access to a wealth of digital resources, including digitized books, manuscripts, and other materials relevant to New York State genealogy.

- Online Databases: Members can access a variety of online databases that contain millions of records unique to New York families, including cemetery records, probate records, and more.

Education and Support
- Educational Programs: The NYG&B organizes a wide range of educational programs, including webinars, workshops, and lectures, covering various aspects of genealogical research, with a focus on New York State.

- Publications: It publishes the "New York Genealogical and Biographical Record," a scholarly journal that includes compiled genealogies, source records, and case studies. Additionally, the society publishes guidebooks and research aids.

- Research Services: For those unable to visit New York or who need expert assistance, the NYG&B offers professional research services to help individuals advance their family history research.

Community Engagement

- Special Interest Groups: The society hosts events and provides forums for special interest groups focusing on specific New York regions or topics in genealogy, fostering a community of like-minded individuals.

- Annual Conference: The NYG&B hosts an annual conference featuring a range of sessions led by notable genealogists, offering networking opportunities and advanced learning experiences.

Membership and Volunteer Opportunities

- Membership is open to anyone interested in New York genealogy, providing benefits such as access to exclusive resources, discounts on publications and events, and opportunities to contribute to society projects.

Preservation and Advocacy

- The NYG&B actively participates in preserving New York's genealogical heritage and advocates for access to public records, playing a crucial role in ensuring that important historical and genealogical resources remain accessible for future generations.

The New York Genealogical and Biographical Society exemplifies the role of state genealogical societies in supporting genealogical research at a state level. Through its comprehensive resources, educational initiatives, and community-building activities, the NYG&B significantly contributes to the field of genealogy, particularly for those tracing their ancestors in New York State.

Texas

Another example is the Texas State Genealogical Society (TxSGS), established in 1960, is a premier organization dedicated to promoting genealogy, family history research, and the preservation of genealogical records in the state of Texas. As a statewide society, TxSGS serves as a hub for individuals and organizations interested in Texas genealogy, offering a wide range of resources, educational opportunities, and support to both novice and experienced researchers. Here's a closer look at what the Texas State Genealogical Society offers:

Mission and Objectives

- Promotion of Genealogical Research: TxSGS aims to encourage and elevate genealogical research standards within Texas, offering tools and guidance to help individuals accurately trace their ancestries.

- Preservation of Records: A key objective is the preservation of Texas's genealogical and historical records, ensuring they remain accessible for future generations.

- Educational Programs: The society is committed to educating the public about genealogical research techniques and the importance of preserving family histories and records.

Resources and Activities

- Publications: TxSGS publishes various materials beneficial to genealogical research, including the "Stirpes", a quarterly journal that features articles on Texas family histories, genealogical records, and research methodologies.

- Annual Conference: One of the highlights of TxSGS's activities is its annual state conference, which gathers genealogists from across the state and beyond for workshops, lectures, and networking opportunities focused on genealogical research and preservation.

- Awards and Scholarships: The society recognizes significant contributions to the field of genealogy and supports the educational pursuits of its members through awards and scholarships.

Membership Benefits

- Members of TxSGS gain access to a wealth of resources, including exclusive online databases, digital archives, and publications. Membership also offers discounts on conference registration fees and access to member-only content and webinars.

Community Engagement and Support

- County Partnerships: TxSGS partners with county genealogical societies across Texas to promote local research projects and events, fostering a statewide network of genealogy enthusiasts and experts.

- Research Assistance: Through its website and publications, TxSGS provides valuable research assistance, offering tips, guides, and access to records that can aid in genealogical research.

- Advocacy: The society also plays a role in advocating for the preservation of public access to historical and genealogical records, ensuring that researchers can continue to access vital information for their work.

Educational Outreach

- TxSGS conducts webinars, workshops, and seminars aimed at enhancing the research skills of its members and the general public. These educational initiatives cover a wide range of topics, from beginner genealogy to more advanced research techniques.

The Texas State Genealogical Society serves as a cornerstone of the genealogical community in Texas, providing essential support and resources to those interested in exploring their family history within the state. Through its efforts in preservation, education, and community engagement, TxSGS plays a critical role in fostering the growth and development of genealogical research in Texas.

Community Genealogical Societies

A community genealogy society operates at a local level, focusing on genealogical research and history within a specific community, town, or county. These societies are vital for people interested in uncovering their ancestry, particularly for those whose families have long-standing ties to a specific area. Here's a closer look at the characteristics and functions of a community genealogy society:

Mission and Goals

- Community Focus: The primary mission is to promote the study of genealogy and local history, helping members and the public trace family lineages and understand the historical context of their ancestors' lives within a specific community.

- Preservation: To collect, preserve, and index local historical and genealogical records, including personal documents, photographs, cemetery records, and local government archives.

Activities and Services

- Resource Library: Many community genealogy societies maintain a library or collection of local historical and genealogical resources, such as city directories, school records, church records, and local newspapers.

- Research Assistance: They often offer research assistance or guidance to members and sometimes the general public, helping navigate local records and providing expertise on local history.

- Meetings and Workshops: Regular meetings and workshops provide opportunities for learning and sharing genealogical research techniques, with a focus on local sources and history.

- Publications: Some societies publish newsletters, journals, or compilations of local records to disseminate information about local families, historical events, and genealogical research findings.

- Online Resources: An increasing number of community genealogy societies offer online databases, digital archives, or forums, facilitating access to local genealogical information and enabling members to share research and connect with distant relatives.

Membership

- Membership is typically open to anyone with an interest in genealogy, regardless of their level of experience. Members benefit from access to society resources, participation in society events, and connections with fellow genealogy enthusiasts.

- Societies often rely on membership dues, donations, and volunteers to support their activities and resource collections.

Community Engagement

- Collaboration: Community genealogy societies frequently collaborate with local libraries, historical societies, and archives to preserve and make accessible historical records.

- Projects: They may engage in projects such as cemetery transcriptions, historical marker placements, and the digitization of local records, contributing to the preservation of community history and heritage.

- Education: By organizing public lectures, exhibits, and genealogy fairs, these societies play an educational role in the community, raising awareness of local history and encouraging the preservation of family histories.

Contribution to Genealogical Research

- Community genealogy societies are invaluable for genealogical researchers, particularly those researching ancestors from specific locales. Their focused collections and local expertise provide insights and access to records not available elsewhere.

- They foster a sense of community among people with shared interests in history and genealogy, providing a supportive environment for exchanging information and assisting each other in research endeavors.

In summary, community genealogy societies are grassroots organizations that play a crucial role in preserving local history and assisting individuals in genealogical research. They offer specialized resources, foster educational opportunities, and build a community of individuals passionate about discovering and preserving their local heritage.

Community Genealogical Societies (examples)

Seattle Genealogical Society

An example of a community genealogy society is the "Seattle Genealogical Society" (SGS) in Seattle, Washington. This society is dedicated to providing resources, support, and education to individuals researching their family history, with a specific focus on Seattle and the broader Pacific Northwest region. Below is an overview of what the Seattle Genealogical Society offers, exemplifying the activities and services of community genealogy societies:

Mission and Objectives

- SGS aims to promote interest in genealogical research and preserve genealogical records, documents, and artifacts relevant to the Seattle area and its residents.

Resources and Collections

- Library: SGS maintains a specialized library containing a variety of genealogical resources, including books, periodicals, city directories, and family histories, with a strong emphasis on Seattle and Washington state.

- Online Databases: Members and non-members can access a range of online databases through the SGS website, including indexes to local records, obituaries, and cemetery records.

- Special Collections: The society has special collections focusing on specific aspects of Seattle's history and its diverse communities, aiding researchers in tracing ancestors from the region.

Education and Support

- Classes and Workshops: SGS offers a variety of educational programs ranging from beginner to advanced genealogy research techniques, including how to use online databases effectively, understanding DNA testing, and researching immigrant ancestors.

- Seminars and Conferences: The society hosts seminars and conferences featuring well-known speakers and experts in genealogy, providing in-depth learning opportunities on specialized topics.

- Research Assistance: Volunteers and members of the society offer research assistance, helping both members and the public with their genealogical queries and research hurdles.

Community Engagement

- Meetings and Networking: Regular meetings provide opportunities for members to share their research, learn from each other, and find collaboration opportunities.

- Special Interest Groups (SIGs): SGS hosts SIGs focusing on specific areas of interest, such as DNA genealogy, specific ethnic research (e.g., Scandinavian, Irish), and technology in genealogy, allowing members to dive deeper into these subjects.

- Publications: The society publishes a newsletter and a journal that include articles on genealogical research, findings, and stories related to the Seattle area, as well as resources and tips for genealogists.

Projects and Contributions

- Record Preservation and Indexing: SGS undertakes projects to preserve and index historical and genealogical records pertinent to Seattle and the surrounding areas, making these records more accessible to researchers.

- Community Outreach: The society participates in community outreach programs, offering presentations and workshops to schools, libraries, and other organizations to promote the importance of genealogy and historical preservation.

The Seattle Genealogical Society is a prime example of how community genealogy societies function and contribute to the field of genealogy. By focusing on local history and providing specialized resources and support, societies like SGS play a vital role in helping individuals connect with their past and understand their ancestors' lives within the context of their local communities.

Dallas Genealogical Society

An example of a community genealogy society in Texas is the "Dallas Genealogical Society" (DGS). Founded in 1954, DGS is one of the oldest and most active genealogical societies in the state of Texas, dedicated to promoting genealogical research, preserving genealogical records, and providing educational opportunities related to genealogy and family history research. Here's an overview of what the Dallas Genealogical Society offers:

Mission and Objectives

- DGS aims to encourage interest in genealogical research, assist members in their genealogical activities, and preserve and make accessible genealogical, historical, and biographical materials related to Dallas, Texas, and its surrounding areas.

Resources and Collections

- Library Collections: DGS supports the Genealogy Section of the J. Erik Jonsson Central Library in Dallas, which houses an extensive collection of genealogical resources, including books, maps, microfilm, and digital databases, with a focus on Texas, the southern United States, and other areas from which Dallas residents originate.

- Online Databases: Members can access a variety of online resources and databases through the DGS website, including cemetery records, marriage records, and archival materials specific to Dallas and Texas.

Education and Support

- Workshops and Seminars: DGS organizes workshops, seminars, and classes covering a wide range of topics, from beginner genealogy research to more advanced subjects like DNA analysis and using technology in genealogy.

- Special Interest Groups: The society hosts several Special Interest Groups (SIGs) focusing on specific areas of genealogy, such as technology, DNA, African American genealogy, and others, allowing members to delve deeper into these topics.

- Meetings and Speakers: Regular meetings feature speakers who are experts in various fields of genealogy, providing insights and information that can aid members in their research.

Community Engagement

- Publications: DGS publishes a quarterly newsletter, "Pegasus; Journal of the Dallas Genealogical Society," which includes articles on genealogical research, society news, and historical information relevant to Dallas and Texas.

- Record Preservation Projects: The society participates in projects to index and preserve historical records, making them more accessible to researchers. These projects often involve collaboration with local archives, libraries, and other historical institutions.

- Outreach and Collaboration: DGS collaborates with local schools, libraries, and community groups to promote genealogy and history through presentations and educational events.

Membership and Volunteer Opportunities

- DGS offers membership to individuals interested in genealogy, providing benefits such as access to member-only resources, discounts on events and workshops, and opportunities to participate in society projects.

- Members can volunteer in various capacities, contributing to the society's mission and projects, and gaining valuable experience in genealogical research and historical preservation.

The Dallas Genealogical Society exemplifies how community genealogy societies can play a crucial role in supporting genealogical research at a local level. Through its resources, educational programs, and community projects, DGS helps individuals trace their ancestry, connects them with others who have similar interests, and contributes to the preservation of local history.

Resources

This section includes a brief discussion of additional genealogy resources including:

- Magazines
- Books
- Digitized Genealogy Books
- Maps
- Public Libraries
- Family Stories

Magazines

Family Tree Magazine
Family Tree Magazine is published in the United States and it offers a wealth of printed and digital material as well as courses and podcasts.

Books

Family History 101, A Beginner's Guide to Finding Your Ancestors, Marcia D. Yannizze Melnyk, 2005.

Unofficial Guide to FamilySearch.org: How to Find Your Family History on the World's Largest Free Genealogy Website by Dana McCullough. 2020.

Unofficial Guide to Ancestory.com: How to Find Your Family History on the #1 Genealogy Website, Nancy Hendrickson, 2018.

Genealogy Standards: Second Edition Revised, Board for Certification of Genealogists, 2021.

The Everything Guide to Online Genealogy: Trace Your Roots, Share Your History, and Create Your Family Tree, Kinberly Powell, 2014.

The Researcher's Guide to American Genealogy, Val D. Greenwood, 2017

Digitized Genealogy Books

books.google.com (free)
Google books offers free books with respect to copyright laws.

hathitrust.org (free)
This website contains digital copies of original pieces of work. In terms of Davy Crockett, if you go to this website and simply type

in his name, you will find a list of original books and documents related to his life and history. It is a rich resource of detailed information about his life and times and people's impressions of him during his life and after. If you search on your own family name, you may be surprised by what you find.

Maps

Online maps (both new and old) can help you learn more about your ancestors. Maps on The Library of Congress website provide a wealth of information.

Searching old state and township maps can also be very rewarding. One of my favorite discoveries was an old township map which had my great great grandfather's name and his neighbor's names hand written on it. I realized I had attended grade school with children who had those same last names. That tells me that their families lived in the same area as my family for generations.

Public Library

Public libraries can be invaluable resources for genealogy research, offering a range of services, collections, and support to help individuals trace their family histories. Here's how a public library can assist with genealogy research:

1. Access to Specialized Databases
Many public libraries provide free access to paid genealogical databases such as Ancestry.com, MyHeritage, or FamilySearch, which can be expensive for an individual to access on their own. These databases offer billions of historical records, including census data, birth and death certificates, marriage records, and immigration records.

2. Local History Collections
Libraries often have collections focused on the local area's history, including microfilm or digital copies of local newspapers, city directories, property records, and local government archives. These

can provide valuable information about ancestors who lived in the area.

3. Genealogy Reference Materials
Reference sections may include genealogy how-to guides, family history books, local and state histories, military records, and ethnic and religious histories. These materials can offer guidance on research techniques and historical context that can enrich your family history.

4. Special Collections and Archives
Some libraries have special collections or archives that include rare books, manuscripts, letters, diaries, and photographs. These unique materials can provide a glimpse into the daily lives of ancestors and the communities they lived in.

5. Workshops and Classes
Libraries may host workshops, classes, and seminars on genealogy research methods, including how to use genealogical software, interpret DNA results, and properly document findings. These educational opportunities are great for both beginners and experienced researchers.

6. Research Assistance
Librarians and volunteers with expertise in genealogy and local history can provide one-on-one assistance, helping patrons navigate resources, suggest research strategies, and sometimes even assist with interpreting historical documents.

7. Interlibrary Loan Services
If your library does not have a specific book, microfilm, or document needed for your research, it may be able to borrow the item from another library through interlibrary loan services. This can greatly expand the range of materials available to you.

8. Access to Local Genealogical Societies
Libraries often collaborate with local genealogical societies, hosting society meetings and workshops at the library. This can be a

great way to connect with other genealogists, share information, and learn from experienced researchers.

9. Online Resources and Digital Libraries

Many libraries also offer access to digital libraries and online resources, including digitized photographs, maps, and documents that can be accessed from home. These resources can be particularly valuable for researching areas far from where you live.

10. Community Events and Networking

Libraries may organize genealogy fairs or history days, providing opportunities to meet experts, connect with distant relatives, or discover new resources and technologies useful for genealogy research.

Public libraries serve as a gateway to a wealth of information and support for genealogy enthusiasts. They offer not only the tools and resources needed to conduct research but also foster a community of learning and discovery that can make the journey into your family's past both fruitful and rewarding.

Family Stories

Using family stories in genealogy research is a valuable and enriching approach to uncovering your ancestry. These narratives, passed down through generations, often contain kernels of truth and links to the past that official records alone cannot provide. Here's how family stories can be used effectively in genealogy research:

Uncovering Leads and Clues

- Names and Relationships: Stories often mention relatives' names, nicknames, and relationships, providing clues to connecting family members and extending your family tree.

- Locations and Migrations: Tales of where ancestors lived, moved to, or came from can guide research into specific geographical areas, leading to records in those locations.

- Occupations and Achievements: Anecdotes about ancestors'

jobs, accomplishments, or roles in the community can lead to employment records, newspaper articles, or other documents.

Contextualizing Historical Records

- Understanding Ancestors' Lives: Family stories can provide context to the dry facts found in records, offering insights into ancestors' personalities, daily lives, and the times they lived in.

- Evaluating Information: Narratives can help evaluate the accuracy of records and reconcile discrepancies. For instance, if a census record conflicts with a well-documented family story, it may warrant a closer examination of both sources.

Preserving and Recording Stories

- Oral Histories: Conducting interviews with older relatives to record their stories and memories is crucial. These oral histories become invaluable resources for current and future research.

- Documenting Narratives: Writing down or recording stories as you hear them helps preserve them. Include as much detail as possible and note the source of the story.

Cross-Referencing with Historical Records

- Verification: Use family stories as starting points for research, but look for historical records to verify the details. Birth, marriage, death records, immigration documents, and census data can confirm or clarify the stories.

- Expanding the Story: As you find records that correspond to family stories, you may discover additional details or corrections to the narratives, enriching your understanding of your ancestors' lives.

Overcoming Research Challenges

- Breaking Through Brick Walls: Sometimes, family stories can provide the clue needed to overcome a research impasse, such as a previously unknown maiden name or a place of origin.

- Identifying Research Directions: Stories can hint at avenues of research previously unconsidered, like military service that suggests checking military records or an ancestor's involvement in a historic event that leads you to specific archives.

-

Ethical Considerations and Sensitivity
- Respect Privacy: Be mindful of sharing sensitive information from family stories, especially concerning living relatives or recent events.

- Consider the Source: Remember that stories can change over time and may contain biases or inaccuracies. Always approach them as one piece of the puzzle, to be considered alongside other evidence.

Family stories are not only a treasure trove of potential leads and context for genealogical research but also a way to connect more deeply with your ancestors. They add color and texture to the skeletal framework provided by official records, bringing the past to life in a way that numbers and dates alone cannot. By integrating these narratives into your research, you preserve your family's heritage and pass on a richer legacy to future generations.

Family stories are full of content and context of former lives. They give us the warp and weave of our family's fabric. Each thread leads to questions about the author(s) and the context of their lives. We hope to unravel some of these treads within the stories of David Crockett and James P. Crockett III to invite exploration, curiosity, and true connection to your family's stories and ancestors.

Introduction to David Crockett's Autobiography

David "Davy" Crockett (1786-1836) was a 19th-century American folk hero, frontiersman, soldier, and politician. Born in what is now Greene County, Tennessee, Crockett grew up on the American frontier and gained a reputation for his hunting skills and knowledge of the wilderness.

Crockett served as a militia soldier during the Creek War (1813-1814), a conflict between the United States and the Creek Nation, which was part of the larger context of the War of 1812. His military service and stories of his frontier adventures contributed to his fame and the development of his larger-than-life image.

In 1821, Crockett began his political career, serving in the Tennessee State Legislature. He was later elected to the U.S. House of Representatives, where he served from 1827 to 1831 and from 1833 to 1835. As a politician, he was known for his independent spirit, colorful speeches, and opposition to President Andrew Jackson's policies, particularly the Indian Removal Act.

Crockett's fame grew through the publication of numerous books, plays, and almanacs that featured his adventures, often in a highly exaggerated and fictionalized form. These works helped to create the legendary image of Davy Crockett as the "King of the Wild Frontier."

In 1835, after losing his bid for re-election to Congress, Crockett went to Texas to join the fight for independence from Mexico. He took part in the Battle of the Alamo in 1836, where he and the other defenders were ultimately killed by Mexican forces led by General Antonio López de Santa Anna. Crockett's death at the Alamo further cemented his status as an American folk hero and symbol of frontier courage and independence.

Davy Crockett was the fifth of nine children born to John and Rebecca (Hawkins) Crockett. The names of his family are as follows:
1. William Crockett (1780 - 1840)
2. Aaron Crockett (1782 - 1835)
3. Nathan Crockett (1783 -1839)
4. James Patterson Crockett (1784 - 1834)

5. David "Davy" Crockett (1786 -1836)
6. John Crockett Jr. (1787 - 1841)
7. Elizabeth Crockett (1788 - ?)
8. Rebecca Jane Crockett (1796 - ?)
9. Girl Crockett (?)

These siblings were raised on the American frontier, primarily in what is now Tennessee. The family experienced the hardships and challenges common to frontier life, including the need for hunting, farming, and defending their land from Native American attacks. The siblings were exposed to these experiences from a young age, which contributed to David Crockett's skills as a frontiersman and his larger-than-life image as a folk hero.

Davy Crockett was married twice in his life, and thus had two families.

• First Marriage: In 1806, at the age of 20, Davy Crockett married Mary "Polly" Finley. They had three children: John Wesley Crockett, William Finley Crockett, and Margaret Finley Crockett. Unfortunately, Polly died in 1815.

• Second Marriage: After Polly's death, Crockett married Elizabeth Patton in 1815. She was a widow with two children from her previous marriage. Together, Davy and Elizabeth had three more children: Robert Patton Crockett, Rebecca Elvira Crockett, and Matilda Crockett.

So, Crockett had a total of six biological children, three from each marriage. Additionally, he was a stepfather to Elizabeth Patton's two children from her first marriage.

In this book we are particularly focused on the experiences of a younger David Crockett. These experiences and his inner drive led him to become the folk hero and legend we know today. But when a young boy and man, David did not have his legendary status. He became 'Davy' Crockett through a series of 'inflection points' discussed earlier in the introduction from Dr. Don Frasier's insights as a professor of history.

As you read through David's autobiography here, we encourage you to look for those 'inflection points' as we did in the Jimmy Highpockets narrative early in our book. Imagine yourself a young David Crockett with eight siblings, loving parents, a poor family, a harsh and dangerous frontier to grown up in. What were young David's impressions and feelings when his father partnered up with Thomas Galbreath to build a grist mill only to have it and their possessions stripped away be a devastating flood. Then his father's roadside tavern in which a young David worked and met many travelers from all walks of life. David states clearly in this autobiography, "I began to make up my acquaintance with hard times, and a plenty of them." We wonder how these 'hard times' affected him personally, as we wonder the same for Jimmy Highpockets and all the young people growing up on the frontier - poor, hard working, scrapping by, being re-sourceful, and staying close to family. Yet, somehow David turns his circumstances into 'inflection points' to become more than his situation.

Try to imagine the impact on David (~12 years old) when his father hired him out to walk 400 miles on foot with a Dutchman cattle driver, Jacob Siler. As David says, "I set out with a heavy heart, it is true, but I went ahead." Are we beginning to hear the voice in his young head that will show up later in life as a soldier, U.S. Congressman, and on the road in Texas to the Alamo. Again, from his own words we begin to see the narrative he details him-self of the points in his life that heavily influenced him.

Later, as David returns to his family home, we learn of more physical and emotional hardships that speak volumes of his drive, persistence, and perseverance. He was incredibly deter-mined for "...home, poor as it was, ...and it seemed ten times as dear to me as it ever did before." He was both well aware of this family's poverty and bond. He was driven to be part of both.

More stories of his brief time in school, being bullied and am-bushing the bully "...scratching his face to a flitter jig" and the consequences from his father and teacher. Trying to avoid a painful whipping from both led David to run away from home hiring himself and an elder brother out with Jesse Cheek to drive horses to Virginia. After more adventures and more employers, we see David avoiding a direct return to home despite his strong feelings about family and friends, but dreading being whipped by his father. David's experiences shape him into the young social, strapping frontiersman he would become.

What's so remarkable about having David's own narrative (as with Jimmy Highpockets) is the direct insight(s) into his young life. We get to peer into their hopes, fears, and values in a way we can only guess at through historical documents, pictures, or antique items. These personal stories from memories (David was about age 47 when he narrated his autobiography; James P. was about age 64) reveal so much about their adventures and misadventures growing up.

These narratives give us details about the places they grew up, the people they related to, and the physical and economic environment that shaped them. We learn about times David was strong and times he ran away. We learn about how David and James P. stood up for themselves when bullied or looked down upon because of their poverty or lack of education. We learn how they used their wits and ingenuity to obtain and master frontier skills like marksmanship, hunting, and taking care of animals. Mostly we learn how they raised themselves up from very poor childhoods to become men of merit.

Most of all these narratives from two adventuresome Crocketts give us insights into two related men and the points in their lives that moved them towards who they would become. We are grateful to present these narratives together so we might read and reflect on these 'inflection points' in their lives, so we might better see them in our and our children's lives.

So, enjoy David's autobiography in its full version. We have enjoyed seeing some parallels between David and his second great grand nephew, James P's younger lives. You can enjoy David's accounts from the rest of his storied life just two years before he arrived at the Alamo. Given the trajectory of events there in propelling him from folk hero to folk legend, one could offer that the Alamo was David's last 'inflection point.'

Either way we luckily have his stories here in his folksy, aw-shucks style and humor. Reading his words gives a real sense of his down-home charm and charisma. He also does not mince words on his opinions of certain people and political situations in his time. He was direct, far reaching, and likable. His autobiography leaves us with little wonder why he was so popular then as now. Please enjoy his stories and see for yourself how he became known as the "King of the Wild Frontier."

NARRATIVE
OF THE
LIFE OF DAVID CROCKETT,
OF THE STATE OF TENNESSEE.
Leave this rule for others when I'm dead:
Be always sure you are right - THEN GO AHEAD!

WRITTEN BY HIMSELF.
SIXTH EDITION.
Entered according to the Act of Congress, in the year 1834,
By David Crockett,

PREFACE

Fashion is a thing I care mighty little about, except when it hap-
pens to run just exactly according to my own notion; and I was
mighty nigh sending out my book without any preface at all, until
a notion struck me, that perhaps it was necessary to explain a
little the reason why and wherefore I had written it.

Most of authors seek fame, but I seek for justice, -a holier impulse
than ever entered into the ambitious struggles of the votaries of
that fickle, flirting goddess.

A publication has been made to the world, which has done me
much injustice; and the catchpenny errors which it contains, have
been already too long sanctioned by my silence. I don't know the
author of the book—and indeed I don't want to know him; for
after he has taken such a liberty with my name, and made such an
effort to hold me up to public ridicule, he cannot calculate on any
thing but my displeasure. If he had been content to have written his opinions about me, however contemptuous they might
have been, I should have had less reason to complain. But when
he professes to give my narrative (as he often does) in my own
language, and then puts into my mouth such language as would
disgrace even an outlandish African, he must himself be sensible
of the injustice he has done me, and the trick he has played off on
the publick. I have met with hundreds, if not with thousands of
people, who have formed their opinions of my appearance, hab-
its, language, and every thing else from that deceptive work.
They have almost in every instance expressed the most profound

astonishment at finding me in human shape, and with the countenance, appearance, and common feelings of a human being. It is to correct all these false notions, and to do justice to myself, that I have written.

It is certain that the writer of the book alluded to has gathered up many imperfect scraps of information concerning me, as in parts of his work there is some little semblance of truth. But I ask him, if this notice should ever reach his eye, how would he have liked it, if I had treated him so?—if I had put together such a bundle of ridiculous stuff, and headed it with his name, and sent it out upon the world without ever even condescending to ask his permission? To these questions, all upright men must give the same answer. It was wrong; and the desire to make money by it, is no apology for such injustice to a fellow man.

But I let him pass; as my wish is greatly more to vindicate myself, than to condemn him.

In the following pages I have endeavoured to give the reader a plain, honest, homespun account of my state in life, and some few of the difficulties which have attended me along its journey, down to this time. I am perfectly aware, that I have related many small and, as I fear, uninteresting circumstances; but if so, my apology is, that it was rendered necessary by a desire to link the different periods of my life together, as they have passed, from my childhood onward, and thereby to enable the reader to select such parts of it as he may relish most, if, indeed, there is any thing in it which may suit his palate.

I have also been operated on by another consideration. It is this:—I know, that obscure as I am, my name is making a considerable deal of fuss in the world. I can't tell why it is, nor in what it is to end. Go where I will, everybody seems anxious to get a peep at me; and it would be hard to tell which would have the advantage, if I, and the "Government," and "Black Hawk," and a great eternal big caravan of wild varments were all to be showed at the same time in four different parts of any of the big cities in the nation. I am not so sure that I shouldn't get the most custom of any of the crew. There must therefore be something in me, or about me, that attracts attention, which is even mysterious to myself. I can't understand it, and I therefore put all the facts down, leaving the reader free to take his choice of them.

On the subject of my style, it is bad enough, in all conscience, to please critics, if that is what they are after. They are a sort of vermin, though, that I sha'n't even so much as stop to brush off. If they want to work on my book, just let them go ahead; and after they are done, they had better blot out all their criticisms, than to know what opinion I would express of them, and by what sort of a curious name I would call them, if I was standing near them, and looking over their shoulders. They will, at most, have only their trouble for their pay. But I rather expect I shall have them on my side.

But I don't know of any thing in my book to be criticised on by honourable men. Is it on my spelling?—that's not my trade. Is it on my grammar?—I hadn't time to learn it, and make no pretensions to it. Is it on the order and arrangement of my book?—I never wrote one before, and never read very many; and, of course, know mighty little about that. Will it be on the authorship of the book?—this I claim, and I'll hang on to it, like a wax plaster. The whole book is my own, and every sentiment and sentence in it. I would not be such a fool, or knave either, as to deny that I have had it hastily run over by a friend or so, and that some little alterations have been made in the spelling and grammar; and I am not so sure that it is not the worse of even that, for I despise this way of spelling contrary to nature. And as for grammar, it's pretty much a thing of nothing at last, after all the fuss that's made about it. In some places, I wouldn't suffer either the spelling, or grammar, or any thing else to be touch'd; and therefore it will be found in my own way.

But if any body complains that I have had it looked over, I can only say to him, her, or them—as the case may be—that while critics were learning grammar, and learning to spell, I, and "Doctor Jackson, L.L.D." were fighting in the wars; and if our books, and messages, and proclamations, and cabinet writings, and so forth, and so on, should need a little looking over, and a little correcting of the spelling and the grammar to make them fit for use, its just nobody's business. Big men have more important matters to attend to than crossing their t's—, and dotting their i's—, and such like small things. But the "Government's" name is to the proclamation, and my name's to the book; and if I didn't write the book, the "Government" didn't write the proclamation, which no man dares to deny!

But just read for yourself, and my ears for a heel tap, if before you get through you don't say, with many a good-natured smile and hearty laugh, "This is truly the very thing itself—the exact image of its Author, David Crockett

Washington City,

February 1st, 1834.

NARRATIVE OF THE
LIFE OF DAVID CROCKETT.

CHAPTER I

As the public seem to feel some interest in the history of an individual so humble as I am, and as that history can be so well known to no person living as to myself, I have, after so long a time, and under many pressing solicitations from my friends and acquaintances, at last determined to put my own hand to it, and lay before the world a narrative on which they may at least rely as being true. And seeking no ornament or colouring for a plain, simple tale of truth, I throw aside all hypocritical and fawning apologies, and, according to my own maxim, just "go ahead." Where I am not known, I might, perhaps, gain some little credit by having thrown around this volume some of the flowers of learning; but where I am known, the vile cheatery would soon be detected, and like the foolish jackdaw, that with a borrowed tail attempted to play the peacock, I should be justly robbed of my pilfered ornaments, and sent forth to strut without a tail for the balance of my time. I shall commence my book with what little I have learned of the history of my father, as all great men rest many, if not most, of their hopes on their noble ancestry. Mine was poor, but I hope honest, and even that is as much as many a man can say. But to my subject.

My father's name was John Crockett, and he was of Irish descent. He was either born in Ireland or on a passage from that country to America across the Atlantic. He was by profession a farmer, and spent the early part of his life in the state of Pennsylvania. The name of my mother was Rebecca Hawkins. She was an American woman, born in the state of Maryland, between York and Baltimore. It is likely I may have heard where they were married, but if so, I have forgotten. It is, however, certain that they were, or else the public would never have been troubled with the history of David Crockett, their son.

I have an imperfect recollection of the part which I have understood my father took in the revolutionary war. I personally know nothing about it, for it happened to be a little before my day; but from himself, and many others who were well acquainted with its troubles and afflictions, I have learned that he was a soldier in the revolutionary war, and took part in that bloody struggle. He fought, according to my information, in the battle at Kings Mountain against the British and tories, and in some other engagements of which my remembrance is too imperfect to enable me to speak with any certainty. At some time, though I cannot say certainly when, my father, as I have understood, lived in Lincoln county, in the state of North Carolina. How long, I don't know. But when he removed from there, he settled in that district of country which is now embraced in the east division of Tennessee, though it was not then erected into a state.

He settled there under dangerous circumstances, both to himself and his family, as the country was full of Indians, who were at that time very troublesome. By the Creeks, my grandfather and grandmother Crockett were both murdered, in their own house, and on the very spot of ground where Rogersville, in Hawkins county, now stands. At the same time, the Indians wounded Joseph Crockett, a brother to my father, by a ball, which broke his arm; and took James a prisoner, who was still a younger brother than Joseph, and who, from natural defects, was less able to make his escape, as he was both deaf and dumb. He remained with them for seventeen years and nine months, when he was discovered and recollected by my father and his eldest brother, William Crockett; and was purchased by them from an Indian trader, at a price which I do not now remember; but so it was, that he was delivered up to them, and they returned him to his relatives. He now lives in Cumberland county, in the state of Kentucky, though I have not seen him for many years.

My father and mother had six sons and three daughters. I was the fifth son. What a pity I hadn't been the seventh! For then I might have been, by common consent, called doctor, as a heap of people get to be great men. But, like many of them, I stood no chance to become great in any other way than by accident. As my father was very poor, and living as he did far back in the back woods, he had neither the means nor the opportunity to give me, or any of the rest of his children, any learning.

But before I get on the subject of my own troubles, and a great many very funny things that have happened to me, like all other historians and biographers, I should not only inform the public that I was born, myself, as well as other folks, but that this important event took place, according to the best information I have received on the subject, on the 17th of August, in the year 1786; whether by day or night, I believe I never heard, but if I did I, have forgotten. I suppose, however, it is not very material to my present purpose, nor to the world, as the more important fact is well attested, that I was born; and, indeed, it might be inferred, from my present size and appearance, that I was pretty well born, though I have never yet attached myself to that numerous and worthy society.

At that time my father lived at the mouth of Lime Stone, on the Nola-chucky river; and for the purpose not only of showing what sort of a man I now am, but also to show how soon I began to be a sort of a little man, I have endeavoured to take the back track of life, in order to fix on the first thing that I can remember. But even then, as now, so many things were happening, that as Major Jack Downing would say, they are all in "a pretty considerable of a snarl," and I find it "kinder hard" to fix on that thing, among them all, which really happened first. But I think it likely, I have hit on the outside line of my recollection; as one thing happened at which I was so badly scared, that it seems to me I could not have forgotten it, if it had happened a little time only after I was born. Therefore it furnishes me with no certain evidence of my age at the time; but I know one thing very well, and that is, that when it happened, I had no knowledge of the use of breeches, for I had never had any nor worn any.

But the circumstance was this: My four elder brothers, and a well-grown boy of about fifteen years old, by the name of Campbell, and myself, were all playing on the river's side; when all the rest of them got into my father's canoe, and put out to amuse themselves on the water, leaving me on the shore alone.

Just a little distance below them, there was a fall in the river, which went slap-right straight down. My brothers, though they were little fellows, had been used to paddling the canoe, and could have carried it safely anywhere about there; but this fellow Campbell wouldn't let them have the paddle, but, fool like, undertook to manage it himself. I reckon he had never seen a water craft before; and it went just any way but the way he wanted it. There he paddled, and paddled, and paddled—all the while going wrong,—until, in a short time, here they were all going, straight forward, stern foremost, right plump to the falls; and if they had only had a fair shake, they would have gone over as slick as a whistle. It was'ent this, though, that scared me; for I was so infernal mad that they had left me on the shore, that I had as soon have seen them all go over the falls a bit, as any other way. But their danger was seen by a man by the name of Kendall, but I'll be shot if it was Amos; for I believe I would know him yet if I was to see him. This man Kendall was working in a field on the bank, and knowing there was no time to lose, he started full tilt, and here he come like a cane brake afire; and as he ran, he threw off his coat, and then his jacket, and then his shirt, for I know when he got to the water he had nothing on but his breeches. But seeing him in such a hurry, and tearing off his clothes as he went, I had no doubt but that the devil or something else was after him—and close on him, too—as he was running within an inch of his life. This alarmed me, and I screamed out like a young painter. But Kendall didn't stop for this. He went ahead with all might, and as full bent on saving the boys, as Amos was on moving the deposites. When he came to the water he plunged in, and where it was too deep to wade he would swim, and where it was shallow enough he went bolting on; and by such exertion as I never saw at any other time in my life, he reached the canoe, when it was within twenty or thirty feet of the falls; and so great was the suck, and so swift the current, that poor Kendall had a hard time of it to stop them at last, as Amos will to stop the mouths of the people

124

about his stockjobbing. But he hung on to the canoe, till he got
it stop'd, and then draw'd it out of danger. When they got out, I
found the boys were more scared than I had been, and the only
thing that comforted me was, the belief that it was a punishment
on them for leaving me on shore.

Shortly after this, my father removed, and settled in the same
county, about ten miles above Greenville.

There another circumstance happened, which made a lasting
impression on my memory, though I was but a small child. Joseph
Hawkins, who was a brother to my mother, was in the woods
hunting for deer. He was passing near a thicket of brush, in which
one of our neighbours was gathering some grapes, as it was in
the fall of the year, and the grape season. The body of the man
was hid by the brush, and it was only as he would raise his hand
to pull the bunches, that any part of him could be seen. It was a
likely place for deer; and my uncle, having no suspicion that it
was any human being, but supposing the raising of the hand to
be the occasional twitch of a deer's ear, fired at the lump, and as
the devil would have it, unfortunately shot the man through the
body. I saw my father draw a silk handkerchief through the bullet hole, and entirely through his body; yet after a while he got
well, as little as any one would have thought it. What become of
him, or whether he is dead or alive, I don't know; but I reckon he
did'ent fancy the business of gathering grapes in an out-of-the-
way thicket soon again.

The next move my father made was to the mouth of Cove creek,
where he and a man by the name of Thomas Galbreath undertook
to build a mill in partnership. They went on very well with their
work until it was nigh done, when there came the second epistle
to Noah's fresh, and away went their mill, shot, lock, and barrel. I
remember the water rose so high, that it got up into the house we
lived in, and my father moved us out of it, to keep us from being
drowned. I was now about seven or eight years old, and have a
pretty distinct recollection of every thing that was going on. From
his bad luck in that business, and being ready to wash out from
mill building, my father again removed, and this time settled in
Jefferson county, now in the state of Tennessee; where he opened
a tavern on the road from Abbingdon to Knoxville.

His tavern was on a small scale, as he was poor; and the principal accommodations which he kept, were for the waggoners who travelled the road. Here I remained with him until I was twelve years old; and about that time, you may guess, if you belong to Yankee land, or reckon, if like me you belong to the back-woods, that I began to make up my acquaintance with hard times, and a plenty of them.

An old Dutchman, by the name of Jacob Siler, who was moving from Knox county to Rockbridge, in the state of Virginia, in passing, made a stop at my father's house. He had a large stock of cattle, that he was carrying on with him; and I suppose made some proposition to my father to hire some one to assist him.

Being hard run every way, and having no thought, as I believe, that I was cut out for a Congressman or the like, young as I was, and as little as I knew about travelling, or being from home, he hired me to the old Dutchman, to go four hundred miles on foot, with a perfect stranger that I never had seen until the evening before. I set out with a heavy heart, it is true, but I went ahead, until we arrived at the place, which was three miles from what is called the Natural Bridge, and made a stop at the house of a Mr. Hartley, who was father-in-law to Mr. Siler, who had hired me. My Dutch master was very kind to me, and gave me five or six dollars, being pleased, as he said, with my services.

This, however, I think was a bait for me, as he persuaded me to stay with him, and not return any more to my father. I had been taught so many lessons of obedience by my father, that I at first supposed I was bound to obey this man, or at least I was afraid openly to disobey him; and I therefore staid with him, and tried to put on a look of perfect contentment until I got the family all to believe I was fully satisfied. I had been there about four or five weeks, when one day myself and two other boys were playing on the road-side, some distance from the house. There came along three waggons. One belonged to an old man by the name of Dunn, and the others to two of his sons. They had each of them a good team, and were all bound for Knoxville. They had been in the habit of stopping at my father's as they passed the road, and I knew them. I made myself known to the old gentleman, and informed him of my situation; I expressed a wish to get back to my father and mother, if they could fix any plan for me to do so. They told me that they would stay that night at a tavern seven miles from there, and that if I could get to them before day the next morning, they would take me home; and if I was pursued, they would protect me. This was a Sunday evening; I went back to the good old Dutchman's house, and as good fortune would have it, he and the family were out on a visit. I gathered my clothes, and what little money I had, and put them all together under the head of my bed. I went to bed early that night, but sleep seemed to be a stranger to me. For though I was a wild boy, yet I dearly loved my father and mother, and their images appeared to be so deeply fixed in my mind, that I could not sleep for thinking of them. And then the fear that when I should attempt to go out, I should be discovered and called to a halt, filled me with anxiety; and between my childish love of home, on the one hand, and the fears of which I have spoken, on the other, I felt mighty queer.

But so it was, about three hours before day in the morning I got up to make my start. When I got out, I found it was snowing fast, and that the snow was then on the ground about eight inches deep. I had not even the advantage of moonlight, and the whole sky was hid by the falling snow, so that I had to guess at my way to the big road, which was about a half mile from the house. I however pushed ahead and soon got to it, and then pursued it, in the direction to the waggons.

I could not have pursued the road if I had not guided myself by the opening it made between the timber, as the snow was too deep to leave any part of it to be known by either seeing or feeling.

Before I overtook the waggons, the earth was covered about as deep as my knees; and my tracks filled so briskly after me, that by daylight, my Dutch master could have seen no trace which I left. I got to the place about an hour before day. I found the waggoners already stirring, and engaged in feeding and preparing their horses for a start. Mr. Dunn took me in and treated me with great kindness. My heart was more deeply impressed by meeting with such a friend, and "at such a time," than by wading the snow-storm by night, or all the other sufferings which my mind had endured. I warmed myself by the fire, for I was very cold, and after an early breakfast, we set out on our journey. The thoughts of home now began to take the entire possession of my mind, and I almost numbered the sluggish turns of the wheels, and much more certainly the miles of our travel, which appeared to me to count mighty slow. I continued with my kind protectors, until we got to the house of a Mr. John Cole, on Roanoke, when my impatience became so great, that I determined to set out on foot and go ahead by myself, as I could travel twice as fast in that way as the waggons could.

Mr. Dunn seemed very sorry to part with me, and used many arguments to prevent me from leaving him. But home, poor as it was, again rushed on my memory, and it seemed ten times as dear to me as it ever had before. The reason was, that my parents were there, and all that I had been accustomed to in the hours of childhood and infancy was there; and there my anxious little heart panted also to be. We remained at Mr. Coles that night, and early in the morning I felt that I couldn't stay; so, taking leave of my friends the waggoners, I went forward on foot, until I was fortunately overtaken by a gentleman, who was returning from market, to which he had been with a drove of horses. He had a led horse, with a bridle and saddle on him, and he kindly offered to let me get on his horse and ride him. I did so, and was glad of the chance, for I was tired, and was, moreover, near the first crossing of Roanoke, which I would have been compelled to wade, cold as the water was, if I had not fortunately met this good man. I travelled with him in this way, without any thing turning up worth recording, until we got within fifteen miles of my father's house. There we parted, and he went on to Kentucky and I trudged on homeward, which place I reached that evening. The name of this kind gentleman I have entirely forgotten, and I am sorry for it; for it deserves a high place in my little book. A remembrance of his kindness to a little straggling boy, and a stranger to him, has however a resting place in my heart, and there it will remain as long as I live.

CHPTER II.

Having gotten home, as I have just related, I remained with my father until the next fall, at which time he took it into his head to send me to a little country school, which was kept in the neighbourhood by a man whose name was Benjamin Kitchen; though I believe he was no way connected with the cabinet. I went four days, and had just began to learn my letters a little, when I had an unfortunate falling out with one of the scholars,—a boy much larger and older than myself. I knew well enough that though the school-house might do for a still hunt, it wouldn't do for a drive, and so I concluded to wait until I could get him out, and then I was determined to give him salt and vinegar. I waited till in the evening, and when the larger scholars were spelling, I slip'd out, and going some distance along his road, I lay by the way-side in the bushes, waiting for him to come along. After a while he and his company came on sure enough, and I pitched out from the bushes and set on him like a wild cat. I scratched his face all to a flitter jig, and soon made him cry out for quarters in good earnest. The fight being over, I went on home, and the next morning was started again to school; but do you think I went? No, indeed. I was very clear of it; for I expected the master would lick me up, as bad as I had the boy. So, instead of going to the school-house, I laid out in the woods all day until in the evening the scholars were dismissed, and my brothers, who were also going to school, came along, returning home. I wanted to conceal this whole business from my father, and I therefore persuaded them not to tell on me, which they agreed to.

Things went on in this way for several days; I starting with them to school in the morning, and returning with them in the evening, but lying out in the woods all day. At last, however, the master wrote a note to my father, inquiring why I was not sent to school. When he read this note, he called me up, and I knew very well that I was in a devil of a hobble, for my father had been taking a few horns, and was in a good condition to make the fur fly. He called on me to know why I had not been at school? I told him I was afraid to go, and that the master would whip me; for I knew quite well if I was turned over to this old Kitchen, I should be cooked up to a cracklin, in little or no time. But I soon found that I was not to expect a much better fate at home; for my father told me, in a very angry manner, that he would whip me an eternal sight worse than the master, if I didn't start immediately to the school. I tried again to beg off; but nothing would do, but to go to the school. Finding me rather too slow about starting, he gathered about a two year old hickory, and broke after me. I put out with all my might, and soon we were both up to the top of our speed. We had a tolerable tough race for about a mile; but mind me, not on the school-house road, for I was trying to get as far the t'other way as possible. And I yet believe, if my father and the school-master could both have levied on me about that time, I should never have been called on to sit in the councils of the nation, for I think they would have used me up. But fortunately for me, about this time, I saw just before me a hill, over which I made headway, like a young steamboat. As soon as I had passed over it, I turned to one side, and hid myself in the bushes. Here I waited until the old gentleman passed by, puffing and blowing, as tho' his steam was high enough to burst his boilers. I waited until he gave up the hunt, and passed back again: I then cut out, and went to the house of an acquaintance a few miles off, who was just about to start with a drove. His name was Jesse Cheek, and I hired my-self to go with him, determining not to return home, as home and the school-house had both become too hot for me. I had an elder brother, who also hired to go with the same drove. We set out and went on through Abbingdon, and the county seat of Withe county, in the state of Virginia; and then through Lynchburgh, by Orange court-house, and Charlottesville, passing through what was called Chester Gap, on to a town called Front Royal, where my employer sold out his drove to a man by the name of Vanmetre; and I was started homeward again, in company with a brother of the first owner of the drove, with one horse between us; having left my brother to come on with the balance of the company.

I traveled on with my new comrade about three days' journey; but much to his discredit, as I then thought, and still think, he took care all the time to ride, but never to tie; at last I told him to go ahead, and I would come when I got ready. He gave me four dollars to bear my expenses upwards of four hundred miles, and then cut out and left me.

I purchased some provisions, and went on slowly, until at length I fell in with a waggoner, with whom I was disposed to scrape up a hasty acquaintance. I inquired where he lived, and where he was going, and all about his affairs. He informed me that he lived in Greenville, Tennessee, and was on his way to a place called Gerardstown, fifteen miles below Winchester. He also said, that after he should make his journey to that place, he would immediately return to Tennessee. His name was Adam Myers, and a jolly good fellow he seemed to be. On a little reflection, I determined to turn back and go with him, which I did; and we journeyed on slowly as waggons commonly do, but merrily enough. I often thought of home, and, indeed, wished bad enough to be there; but, when I thought of the school-house, and Kitchen, my master, and the race with my father, and the big hickory he carried, and of the fierceness of the storm of wrath that I had left him in, I was afraid to venture back; for I knew my father's nature so well, that I was certain his anger would hang on to him like a turtle does to a fisherman's toe, and that, if I went back in a hurry, he would give me the devil in three or four ways But I and the waggoner had traveled two days, when we met my brother, who, I before stated, I had left behind when the drove was sold out. He persuaded me to go home, but I refused. He pressed me hard, and brought up a great many mighty strong arguments to induce me to turn back again. He pictured the pleasure of meeting my mother, and my sisters, who all loved me dearly, and told me what uneasiness they had already suffered about me. I could not help shedding tears, which I did not often do, and my affections all pointed back to those dearest friends, and as I thought, nearly the only ones I had in the world; but then the promised whipping—that was the thing. It came right slap down on every thought of home; and I finally determined that make or break, hit or miss, I would just hang on to my journey, and go ahead with the waggoner. My brother was much grieved at our parting, but he went his way, and so did I. We went on until at last we got to Gerardstown, where the waggoner tried to get a back load, but he could not without going to Alexandria. He engaged to go there, and I concluded that I would wait until he returned. I set in to work for a man by the name of John Gray, at twenty-five cents per day. My labour, however, was light, such as ploughing in some small grain, in which I succeeded in pleasing the old man very well. I continued working for him until the waggoner got back, and for a good long time afterwards, as he continued to run his team back and forward, hauling to and from Baltimore. In the next spring, from the proceeds of my daily labour, small as it was, I was able to get me some decent clothes, and concluded I would make a trip with the waggoner to Baltimore, and see what sort of a place that was, and what sort of folks lived there. I gave him the balance of what money I had for safe keeping, which, as well as I recollect, was about seven dollars. We got on well enough until we came near Ellicott's Mills. Our load consisted of flour, in barrels. Here I got into the waggon for the purpose of changing my clothing, not thinking that I was in any danger; but while I was in there we were met by some wheel-barrow men, who were working on the road, and the horses took a scare and away they went, like they had seen a ghost. They made a sudden wheel around, and broke the waggon tongue slap, short off, as a pipe-stem; and snap went both of the axletrees at the same time, and of all devlish flouncing about of flour barrels that ever was seen, I reckon this took the beat. Even a rat would have stood a bad chance in a straight race among them, and not much better in a crooked one; for he would have been in a good way to be ground up as fine as ginger by their rolling over him. But this proved to me, that if a fellow is born to be hung, he will never be drowned; and, further, that if he is born for a seat in Congress, even flour barrels can't make a mash of him. All these dangers I escaped unhurt, though, like most of the office-holders of these times, for a while I was afraid to say my soul was my own; for I didn't know how soon I should be knocked into a cocked hat, and get my walking papers for another country.

We put our load into another waggon, and hauled ours to a work-man's shop in Baltimore, having delivered the flour, and there we intended to remain two or three days, which time was necessary to repair the runaway waggon. While I was there, I went, one day, down to the wharf, and was much delighted to see the big ships, and their sails all flying; for I had never seen any such things be-fore, and, indeed, I didn't believe there were any such things in all nature. After a short time my curiosity induced me to step aboard of one, where I was met by the captain, who asked me if I didn't wish to take a voyage to London? I told him I did, for by this time I had become pretty well weaned from home, and I cared but little where I was, or where I went, or what become of me. He said he wanted just such a boy as I was, which I was glad to hear. I told him I would go and get my clothes, and go with him. He enquired about my parents, where they lived, and all about them. I let him know that they lived in Tennessee, many hundred miles off. We soon agreed about my intended voyage, and I went back to my friend, the waggoner, and informed him that I was going to London, and wanted my money and my clothes. He refused to let me have either, and swore that he would confine me, and take me back to Tennessee. I took it to heart very much, but he kept so close and constant a watch over me, that I found it impossible to escape from him, until he had started homeward, and made several days' journey on the road. He was, during this time, very ill to me, and threatened me with his waggon whip on several occasions. At length I resolved to leave him at all hazards; and so, before day, one morning, I got my clothes out of his waggon, and cut out, on foot, without a farthing of money to bear my expenses. For all other friends having failed, I determined then to throw myself on Providence, and see how that would use me. I had gone, however, only a few miles when I came up with another waggoner, and such was my situation, that I felt more than ever the necessity of endeavouring to find a friend. I therefore concluded I would seek for one in him. He was going westwardly, and very kindly enquired of me where I was travelling? My youthful resolution, which had brooked almost every thing else, rather gave way at this enquiry; for it brought the loneliness of my situation, and every thing else that was calculated to oppress me, directly to view. My first answer to his question was in a sprinkle of tears, for if the world had been given to me, I could not, at that moment, have helped crying. As soon as the storm of feeling was over, I told him how I had been treated by the waggoner but a little before, who kept what little money I had, and left me without a copper to buy even a morsel of food.

He became exceedingly angry, and swore that he would make the other waggoner give up my money, pronouncing him a scoundrel, and many other hard names. I told him I was afraid to see him, for he had threatened me with his waggon whip, and I believed he would injure me. But my new friend was a very large, stout-looking man, and as resolute as a tiger. He bid me not to be afraid, still swearing he would have my money, or whip it out of the wretch who had it.

We turned and went back about two miles, when we reached the place where he was. I went reluctantly; but I depended on my friend for protection. When we got there, I had but little to say; but approaching the waggoner, my friend said to him, "You damn'd rascal, you have treated this boy badly." To which he replied, it was my fault. He was then asked, if he did not get seven dollars of my money, which he confessed. It was then demanded of him; but he declared most solemnly, that he had not that amount in the world; that he had spent my money, and intended paying it back to me when we got to Tennessee. I then felt reconciled, and persuaded my friend to let him alone, and we returned to his waggon, geared up, and started. His name I shall never forget while my memory lasts; it was Henry Myers. He lived in Pennsylvania, and I found him what he professed to be, a faithful friend and a clever fellow.

We traveled together for several days, but at length I concluded to endeavour to make my way homeward; and for that purpose set out again on foot, and alone. But one thing I must not omit. The last night I staid with Mr. Myers, was at a place where several other waggoners also staid. He told them, before we parted, that I was a poor little straggling boy, and how I had been treated; and that I was without money, though I had a long journey before me, through a land of strangers, where it was not even a wilderness. They were good enough to contribute a sort of money-purse, and presented me with three dollars. On this amount I travelled as far as Montgomery court-house, in the state of Virginia, where it gave out. I set in to work for a man by the name of James Caldwell, a month, for five dollars, which was about a shilling a day. When this time was out, I bound myself to a man by the name of Elijah Griffith, by trade a hatter, agreeing to work for him four years. I remained with him about eighteen months, when he found himself so involved in debt, that he broke up, and left the country. For this time I had received nothing, and was, of course, left without money, and with but very few clothes, and them very indifferent ones. I, however, set in again, and worked about as I could catch employment, until I got a little money, and some clothing; and once more cut out for home. When I reached New River, at the mouth of a small stream, called Little River, the white caps were flying so, that I couldn't get any body to attempt to put me across. I argued the case as well as I could, but they told me there was great danger of being capsized, and drowned, if I attempted to cross. I told them if I could get a canoe I would venture, caps or no caps. They tried to persuade me out of it; but finding they could not, they agreed I might take a canoe, and so I did, and put off. I tied my clothes to the rope of the canoe, to have them safe, whatever might happen. But I found it a mighty ticklish business, I tell you. When I got out fairly on the river, I would have given the world, if it had belonged to me, to have been back on shore. But there was no time to lose now, so I just determined to do the best I could, and the devil take the hindmost. I turned the canoe across the waves, to do which, I had to turn it nearly up the river, as the wind came from that way; and I went about two miles before I could land. When I struck land, my canoe was about half full of water, and I was as wet as a drowned rat. But I was so much rejoiced, that I scarcely felt the cold, though my clothes were frozen on me; and in this situation, I had to go above three miles, before I could find any house, or fire to warm at. I, however, made out to get to one at last, and then I thought I would warm the inside a little, as well as the outside, that there might be no grumbling.

So I took "a leetle of the creater,"—that warmer of the cold, and cooler of the hot,—and it made me feel so good that I concluded it was like the negro's rabbit, "good any way." I passed on until I arrived in Sullivan county, in the state of Tennessee, and there I met with my brother, who had gone with me when I started from home with the cattle drove.

I staid with him a few weeks, and then went on to my father's, which place I reached late in the evening. Several waggons were there for the night, and considerable company about the house. I enquired if I could stay all night, for I did not intend to make myself known, until I saw whether any of the family would find me out. I was told that I could stay, and went in, but had mighty little to say to any body. I had been gone so long, and had grown so much, that the family did not at first know me. And another, and perhaps a stronger reason was, they had no thought or expectation of me, for they all had long given me up for finally lost. After a while, we were all called to supper. I went with the rest. We had sat down to the table and begun to eat, when my eldest sister recollected me: she sprung up, ran and seized me around the neck, and exclaimed, "Here is my lost brother."

My feelings at this time it would be vain and foolish for me to attempt to describe. I had often thought I felt before, and I suppose I had, but sure I am, I never had felt as I then did. The joy of my sisters and my mother, and, indeed, of all the family, was such that it humbled me, and made me sorry that I hadn't submitted to a hundred whippings, sooner than cause so much affliction as they had suffered on my account. I found the family had never heard a word of me from the time my brother left me. I was now almost fifteen years old; and my increased age and size, together with the joy of my father, occasioned by my unexpected return, I was sure would secure me against my long dreaded whipping; and so they did. But it will be a source of astonishment to many, who reflect that I am now a member of the American Congress,—the most enlightened body of men in the world,—that at so advanced an age, the age of fifteen, I did not know the first letter in the book.

CHAPTER III.

I had remained for some short time at home with my father, when he informed me that he owed a man, whose name was Abraham Wilson, the sum of thirty-six dollars, and that if I would set in and work out the note, so as to lift it for him, he would discharge me from his service, and I might go free. I agreed to do this, and went immediately to the man who held my father's note, and contracted with him to work six months for it. I set in, and worked with all my might, not losing a single day in the six months. When my time was out, I got my father's note, and then declined working with the man any longer, though he wanted to hire me mighty bad. The reason was, it was a place where a heap of bad company met to drink and gamble, and I wanted to get away from them, for I know'd very well if I staid there, I should get a bad name, as nobody could be respectable that would live there. I therefore returned to my father, and gave him up his paper, which seemed to please him mightily, for though he was poor, he was an honest man, and always tried mighty hard to pay off his debts.

I next went to the house of an honest old Quaker, by the name of John Kennedy, who had removed from North Carolina, and proposed to hire myself to him, at two shillings a day. He agreed to take me a week on trial; at the end of which he appeared pleased with my work, and informed me that he held a note on my father for forty dollars, and that he would give me that note if I would work for him six months. I was certain enough that I should never get any part of the note; but then I remembered it was my father that owed it, and I concluded it was my duty as a child to help him along, and ease his lot as much as I could. I told the Quaker I would take him up at his offer, and immediately went to work. I never visited my father's house during the whole time of this engagement, though he lived only fifteen miles off. But when it was finished, and I had got the note, I borrowed one of my employer's horses, and, on a Sunday evening, went to pay my parents a visit. Some time after I got there, I pulled out the note and handed it to my father, who supposed Mr. Kennedy had sent it for collection. The old man looked mighty sorry, and said to me he had not the money to pay it, and didn't know what he should do. I then told him I had paid it for him, and it was then his own; that it was not presented for collection, but as a present from me. At this, he shed a heap of tears; and as soon as he got a little over it, he said he was sorry he couldn't give me any thing, but he was not able, he was too poor.

The next day, I went back to my old friend, the Quaker, and set in to work for him for some clothes; for I had now worked a year without getting any money at all, and my clothes were nearly all worn out, and what few I had left were mighty indifferent. I worked in this way for about two months; and in that time a young woman from North Carolina, who was the Quaker's niece, came on a visit to his house. And now I am just getting on a part of my history that I know I never can forget. For though I have heard people talk about hard loving, yet I reckon no poor devil in this world was ever cursed with such hard love as mine has always been, when it came on me. I soon found myself head over heels in love with this girl, whose name the public could make no use of; and I thought that if all the hills about there were pure chink, and all belonged to me, I would give them if I could just talk to her as I wanted to; but I was afraid to begin, for when I would think of saying any thing to her, my heart would begin to flutter like a duck in a puddle; and if I tried to outdo it and speak, it would get right smack up in my throat, and choak me like a cold potatoe. It bore on my mind in this way, till at last I concluded I must die if I didn't broach the subject; and so I determined to begin and hang on a trying to speak, till my heart would get out of my throat one way or t'other. And so one day at it I went, and after several trials I could say a little. I told her how well I loved her; that she was the darling object of my soul and body; and I must have her, or else I should pine down to nothing, and just die away with the consumption.

I found my talk was not disagreeable to her; but she was an honest girl, and didn't want to deceive nobody. She told me she was engaged to her cousin, a son of the old Quaker. This news was worse to me than war, pestilence, or famine; but still I knowed I could not help myself. I saw quick enough my cake was dough, and I tried to cool off as fast as possible; but I had hardly safety pipes enough, as my love was so hot as mighty nigh to burst my boilers. But I didn't press my claims any more, seeing there was no chance to do any thing.

I began now to think, that all my misfortunes growed out of my want of learning. I had never been to school but four days, as the reader has already seen, and did not yet know a letter.

I thought I would try to go to school some; and as the Quaker had a married son, who was living about a mile and a half from him, and keeping a school, I proposed to him that I would go to school four days in the week, and work for him the other two, to pay my board and schooling. He agreed I might come on those terms; and so at it I went, learning and working back and forwards, until I had been with him nigh on to six months. In this time I learned to read a little in my primer, to write my own name, and to cypher some in the three first rules in figures. And this was all the schooling I ever had in my life, up to this day. I should have continued longer, if it hadn't been that I concluded I couldn't do any longer without a wife; and so I cut out to hunt me one.

I found a family of very pretty little girls that I had known when very young. They had lived in the same neighborhood with me, and I had thought very well of them. I made an offer to one of them, whose name is nobody's business, no more than the Quaker girl's was, and I found she took it very well. I still continued paying my respects to her, until I got to love her as bad as I had the Quaker's niece; and I would have agreed to fight a whole regiment of wild cats if she would only have said she would have me. Several months passed in this way, during all of which time she continued very kind and friendly. At last, the son of the old Quaker and my first girl had concluded to bring their matter to a close, and my little queen and myself were called on to wait on them. We went on the day, and performed our duty as attendants. This made me worse than ever; and after it was over, I pressed my claim very hard on her, but she would still give me a sort of an evasive answer. However, I gave her mighty little peace, till she told me at last she would have me. I thought this was glorification enough, even without spectacles. I was then about eighteen years old. We fixed the time to be married; and I thought if that day come, I should be the happiest man in the created world, or in the moon, or any where else.

I had by this time got to be mighty fond of the rifle, and had bought a capital one. I most generally carried her with me where ever I went, and though I had got back to the old Quaker's to live, who was a very particular man, I would sometimes slip out and attend the shooting matches, where they shot for beef; I always tried, though, to keep it a secret from him. He had at the same time a bound boy living with him, who I had gotten into almost as great a notion of the girls as myself. He was about my own age, and was deeply smitten with the sister to my intended wife. I know'd it was in vain to try to get the leave of the old man for my young associate to go with me on any of my courting frolics;

but I thought I could fix a plan to have him along, which would not injure the Quaker, as we had no notion that he should ever know it. We commonly slept up-stairs, and at the gable end of the house there was a window. So one Sunday, when the old man and his family were all gone to meeting, we went out and cut a long pole, and, taking it to the house, we set it up on end in the corner, reaching up the chimney as high as the window. After this we would go up-stairs to bed, and then putting on our Sunday clothes, would go out at the window, and climb down the pole, take a horse apiece, and ride about ten miles to where his sweetheart lived, and the girl I claimed as my wife. I was always mighty careful to be back before day, so as to escape being found out; and in this way I continued my attentions very closely until a few days before I was to be married, or at least thought I was, for I had no fear that any thing was about to go wrong.

Just now I heard of a shooting-match in the neighbourhood, right between where I lived and my girl's house; and I determined to kill two birds with one stone,—to go to the shooting match first, and then to see her. I therefore made the Quaker believe I was going to hunt for deer, as they were pretty plenty about in those parts; but, instead of hunting them, I went straight on to the shooting-match, where I joined in with a partner, and we put in several shots for the beef. I was mighty lucky, and when the match was over I had won the whole beef. This was on a Saturday, and my success had put me in the finest humour in the world. So I sold my part of the beef for five dollars in the real grit, for I believe that was before bank-notes was invented; at least, I had never heard of any. I now started on to ask for my wife; for, though the next Thursday was our wedding day, I had never said a word to her parents about it. I had always dreaded the undertaking so bad, that I had put the evil hour off as long as possible; and, indeed, I calculated they knowed me so well, they wouldn't raise any objection to having me for their son-in-law. I had a great deal better opinion of myself, I found, than other people had of me; but I moved on with a light heart, and my five dollars jingling in my pocket, thinking all the time there was but few greater men in the world than myself.

In this flow of good humour I went ahead, till I got within about two miles of the place, when I concluded I would stop awhile at the house of the girl's uncle; where I might enquire about the family, and so forth, and so on. I was indeed just about ready to consider her uncle, my uncle; and her affairs, my affairs. When I went in, tho', I found her sister there. I asked how all was at home? In a minute I found from her countenance something was wrong. She looked mortified, and didn't answer as quick as I thought she ought, being it was her brother-in-law talking to her. However, I asked her again. She then burst into tears, and told me her sister was going to deceive me; and that she was to be married to another man the next day. This was as sudden to me as a clap of thunder of a bright sunshiny day. It was the cap-stone of all the afflictions I had ever met with; and it seemed to me, that it was more than any human creature could endure. It struck me perfectly speechless for some time, and made me feel so weak, that I thought I should sink down. I however recovered from my shock after a little, and rose and started without any ceremony, or even bidding any body good-bye. The young woman followed me out to the gate, and entreated me to go on to her father's, and said she would go with me. She said the young man, who was going to marry her sister, had got his license, and had asked for her; but she assured me her father and mother both preferred me to him; and that she had no doubt but that, if I would go on, I could break off the match. But I found I could go no further. My heart was bruised, and my spirits were broken down; so I bid her farewell, and turned my lonesome and miserable steps back again homeward, concluding that I was only born for hardships, misery, and disappointment. I now began to think, that in making me, it was entirely forgotten to make my mate; that I was born odd, and should always remain so, and that nobody would have me. But all these reflections did not satisfy my mind, for I had no peace day nor night for several weeks. My appetite failed me, and I grew daily worse and worse. They all thought I was sick; and so I was. And it was the worst kind of sickness,—a sickness of the heart, and all the tender parts, produced by disappointed love.

CHAPTER IV.

I continued in this down-spirited situation for a good long time, until one day I took my rifle and started a hunting. While out, I made a call at the house of a Dutch widow, who had a daughter that was well enough as to smartness, but she was as ugly as a stone fence. She was, however, quite talkative, and soon begun to laugh at me about my disappointment.

She seemed disposed, though, to comfort me as much as she could; and, for that purpose, told me to keep in good heart, that "there was as good fish in the sea as had ever been caught out of it." I doubted this very much; but whether or not, I was certain that she was not one of them, for she was so homely that it almost give me a pain in the eyes to look at her.

But I couldn't help thinking, that she had intended what she had said as a banter for me to court her!!!—the last thing in creation I could have thought of doing. I felt little inclined to talk on the subject, it is true; but, to pass off the time, I told her I thought I was born odd, and that no fellow to me could be found. She protested against this, and said if I would come to their reaping, which was not far off, she would show me one of the prettiest little girls there I had ever seen. She added that the one who had deceived me was nothing to be compared with her. I didn't believe a word of all this, for I had thought that such a piece of flesh and blood as she was had never been manufactured, and never would again. I agreed with her, though, that the little varment had treated me so bad, that I ought to forget her, and yet I couldn't do it. I concluded the best way to accomplish it was to cut out again, and see if I could find any other that would answer me; and so I told the Dutch girl I would be at the reaping, and would bring as many as I could with me.

I employed my time pretty generally in giving information of it, as far as I could, until the day came; and I then offered to work for my old friend, the Quaker, two days, if he would let his bound boy go with me one to the reaping. He refused, and reproved me pretty considerable roughly for my proposition; and said, if he was in my place he wouldn't go; that there would be a great deal of bad company there; and that I had been so good a boy, he would be sorry for me to get a bad name. But I knowed my promise to the Dutch girl, and I was resolved to fulfil it; so I shouldered my rifle, and started by myself. When I got to the place, I found a large company of men and women, and among them an old Irish woman, who had a great deal to say. I soon found out from my Dutch girl, that this old lady was the mother of the little girl she had promised me, though I had not yet seen her. She was in an out-house with some other youngsters, and had not yet made her appearance. Her mamma, however, was no way bashful. She came up to me, and began to praise my red cheeks, and said she had a sweetheart for me. I had no doubt she had been told what I come for, and all about it. In the evening I was introduced to her daughter, and I must confess, I was plaguy well pleased with her from the word go. She had a good countenance, and was very pretty, and I was full bent on making up an acquaintance with her.

It was not long before the dancing commenced, and I asked her to join me in a reel. She very readily consented to do so; and after we had finished our dance, I took a seat alongside of her, and entered into a talk. I found her very interesting; while I was setting by her, making as good a use of my time as I could, her mother came to us, and very jocularly called me her son-in-law. This rather confused me, but I looked on it as a joke of the old lady, and tried to turn it off as well as I could; but I took care to pay as much attention to her through the evening as I could. I went on the old saying, of salting the cow to catch the calf. I soon become so much pleased with this little girl, that I began to think the Dutch girl had told me the truth, when she said there was still good fish in the sea.

We continued our frolic till near day, when we joined in some plays, calculated to amuse youngsters. I had not often spent a more agreeable night. In the morning, however, we all had to part; and I found my mind had become much better reconciled than it had been for a long time. I went home to the Quaker's, and made a bargain to work with his son for a low-priced horse. He was the first one I had ever owned, and I was to work six months for him. I had been engaged very closely five or six weeks, when this little girl run in my mind so, that I concluded I must go and see her, and find out what sort of people they were at home. I mounted my horse and away I went to where she lived, and when I got there I found her father a very clever old man, and the old woman as talkative as ever. She wanted badly to find out all about me, and as I thought to see how I would do for her girl. I had not yet seen her about, and I began to feel some anxiety to know where she was.

In a short time, however, my impatience was relieved, as she arrived at home from a meeting to which she had been. There was a young man with her, who I soon found was disposed to set up claim to her, as he was so attentive to her that I could hardly get to slip in a word edgeways. I began to think I was barking up the wrong tree again; but I was determined to stand up to my rack, fodder or no fodder. And so, to know her mind a little on the subject, I began to talk about starting, as I knowed she would then show some sign, from which I could understand which way the wind blowed. It was then near night, and my distance was fifteen miles home. At this my little girl soon began to indicate to the other gentleman that his room would be the better part of his company. At length she left him, and came to me, and insisted mighty hard that I should not go that evening; and, indeed, from all her actions and the attempts she made to get rid of him, I saw that she preferred me all holler. But it wasn't long before I found trouble enough in another quarter. Her mother was deeply enlisted for my rival, and I had to fight against her influence as well as his. But the girl herself was the prize I was fighting for; and as she welcomed me, I was determined to lay siege to her, let what would happen. I commenced a close courtship, having cornered her from her old beau; while he set off, looking on, like a poor man at a country frolic, and all the time almost gritting his teeth with pure disappointment. But he didn't dare to attempt any thing more, for now I had gotten a start, and I looked at him every once in a while as fierce as a wild-cat. I staid with her until Monday morning, and then I put out for home.

It was about two weeks after this that I was sent for to engage in a wolf hunt, where a great number of men were to meet, with their dogs and guns, and where the best sort of sport was expected. I went as large as life, but I had to hunt in strange woods, and in a part of the country which was very thinly inhabited. While I was out it clouded up, and I began to get scared; and in a little while

144

I was so much so, that I didn't know which way home was, nor any thing about it. I set out the way I thought it was, but it turned out with me, as it always does with a lost man, I was wrong, and took exactly the contrary direction from the right one. And for the information of young hunters, I will just say, in this place, that whenever a fellow gets bad lost, the way home is just the way he don't think it is. This rule will hit nine times out of ten. I went ahead, though, about six or seven miles, when I found night was coming on fast; but at this distressing time I saw a little woman streaking it along through the woods like all wrath, and so I cut on too, for I was determined I wouldn't lose sight of her that night any more. I run on till she saw me, and she stopped; for she was as glad to see me as I was to see her, as she was lost as well as me. When I came up to her, who should she be but my little girl, that I had been paying my respects to. She had been out hunting her father's horses, and had missed her way, and had no knowl-edge where she was, or how far it was to any house, or what way would take us there. She had been travelling all day, and was mighty tired; and I would have taken her up, and toated her, if it hadn't been that I wanted her just where I could see her all the time, for I thought she looked sweeter than sugar; and by this time I loved her almost well enough to eat her.

At last I came to a path, that I know'd must go somewhere, and so we followed it, till we came to a house, at about dark. Here we staid all night. I set up all night courting; and in the morning we parted. She went to her home, from which we were distant about seven miles, and I to mine, which was ten miles off.

I now turned in to work again; and it was about four weeks be-fore I went back to see her. I continued to go occasionally, until I had worked long enough to pay for my horse, by putting in my gun with my work, to the man I had purchased from; and then I began to count whether I was to be deceived again or not. At our next meeting we set the day for our wedding; and I went to my father's, and made arrangements for an infair, and returned to ask her parents for her. When I got there, the old lady appeared to be mighty wrathy; and when I broached the subject, she looked at me as savage as a meat axe. The old man appeared quite willing, and treated me very clever. But I hadn't been there long, before the old woman as good as ordered me out of her house. I thought I would put her in mind of old times, and see how that would go with her. I told her she had called me her son-in-law before I had attempted to call her my mother-in-law and I thought she ought to cool off. But her Irish was up too high to do any thing with her, and so I quit trying. All I cared for was, to have her daughter on my side, which I knowed was the case then; but how soon some other fellow might knock my nose out of joint again, I couldn't tell. I however felt rather insulted at the old lady, and I thought I wouldn't get married in her house. And so I told her girl, that I would come the next Thursday, and bring a horse, bridle, and saddle for her, and she must be ready to go. Her mother declared I shouldn't have her; but I know'd I should, if somebody else didn't get her before Thursday. I then started, bidding them good day, and went by the house of a justice of the peace, who lived on the way to my father's, and made a bargain with him to marry me.

When Thursday came, all necessary arrangements were made at my father's to receive my wife; and so I took my eldest brother and his wife, and another brother, and a single sister that I had, and two other young men with me, and cut out to her father's house to get her. We went on, until we got within two miles of the place, where we met a large company that had heard of the wedding, and were waiting. Some of that company went on with my brother and sister, and the young man I had picked out to wait on me. When they got there, they found the old lady as wrathy as ever. However the old man filled their bottle, and the young men returned in a hurry. I then went on with my company, and when I arrived I never pretended to dismount from my horse, but rode up to the door, and asked the girl if she was ready; and she said she was. I then told her to light on the horse I was leading; and she did so. Her father, though, had gone out to the gate, and when I started he commenced persuading me to stay and marry there; that he was entirely willing to the match, and that his wife, like most women, had entirely too much tongue; but that I oughtn't to mind her. I told him if she would ask me to stay and marry at her house, I would do so. With that he sent for her, and after they had talked for some time out by themselves, she came to me and looked at me mighty good, and asked my pardon for what she had said, and invited me stay. She said it was the first child she had ever had to marry; and she couldn't bear to see her go off in that way; that if I would light, she would do the best she could for us. I couldn't stand every thing, and so I agreed, and we got down, and went in. I sent off then for my parson, and got married in a short time; for I was afraid to wait long, for fear of another defeat. We had as good treatment as could be expected; and that night all went on well. The next day we cut out for my father's, where we met a large company of people, that had been waiting a day and a night for our arrival. We passed the time quite merrily, until the company broke up; and having gotten my wife, I thought I was completely made up, and needed nothing more in the whole world. But I soon found this was all a mistake—for now having a wife, I wanted every thing else; and, worse than all, I had nothing to give for it.

I remained a few days at my father's, and then went back to my new father-in-law's; where, to my surprise, I found my old Irish mother in the finest humour in the world.

She gave us two likely cows and calves, which, though it was a small marriage-portion, was still better than I had expected, and, indeed, it was about all I ever got. I rented a small farm and cabin, and went to work; but I had much trouble to find out a plan to get any thing to put in my house. At this time, my good old friend the Quaker came forward to my assistance, and gave me an order to a store for fifteen dollars' worth of such things as my little wife might choose. With this, we fixed up pretty grand, as we thought, and allowed to get on very well. My wife had a good wheel, and knowed exactly how to use it. She was also a good weaver, as most of the Irish are, whether men or women; and being very industrious with her wheel, she had, in little or no time, a fine web of cloth, ready to make up; and she was good at that too, and at almost any thing else that a woman could do.

We worked on for some years, renting ground, and paying high rent, until I found it wan't the thing it was cracked up to be; and that I couldn't make a fortune at it just at all. So I concluded to quit it, and cut out for some new country. In this time we had two sons, and I found I was better at increasing my family than my fortune. It was therefore the more necessary that I should hunt some better place to get along; and as I knowed I would have to move at some time, I thought it was better to do it before my family got too large, that I might have less to carry.

The Duck and Elk river country was just beginning to settle, and I determined to try that. I had now one old horse, and a couple of two year old colts. They were both broke to the halter, and my father-in-law proposed, that, if I went, he would go with me, and take one horse to help me move. So we all fixed up, and I packed my two colts with as many of my things as they could bear; and away we went across the mountains. We got on well enough, and arrived safely in Lincoln county, on the head of the Mulberry fork of Elk river. I found this a very rich country, and so new, that game, of different sorts, was very plenty. It was here that I began to distinguish myself as a hunter, and to lay the foundation for all my future greatness; but mighty little did I know of what sort it was going to be. Of deer and smaller game I killed abundance; but the bear had been much hunted in those parts before, and were not so plenty as I could have wished. I lived here in the years 1809 and '10, to the best of my recollection, and then I moved to Franklin county, and settled on Beans creek, where I remained till after the close of the last war.

CHAPTER V.

I was living ten miles below Winchester when the Creek war commenced; and as military men are making so much fuss in the world at this time, I must give an account of the part I took in the defence of the country. If it should make me president, why I can't help it; such things will sometimes happen; and my pluck is, never "to seek, nor decline office."

It is true, I had a little rather not; but yet, if the government can't get on without taking another president from Tennessee, to finish the work of "retrenchment and reform," why, then, I reckon I must go in for it. But I must begin about the war, and leave the other matter for the people to begin on.

The Creek Indians had commenced their open hostilities by a most bloody butchery at Fort Mimms. There had been no war among us for so long, that but few, who were not too old to bear arms, knew any thing about the business. I, for one, had often thought about war, and had often heard it described; and I did verily believe in my own mind, that I couldn't fight in that way at all; but my after experience convinced me that this was all a notion. For when I heard of the mischief which was done at the fort, I instantly felt like going, and I had none of the dread of dying that I expected to feel. In a few days a general meeting of the militia was called for the purpose of raising volunteers; and when the day arrived for that meeting, my wife, who had heard me say I meant to go to the war, began to beg me not to turn out. She said she was a stranger in the parts where we lived, had no connexions living near her, and that she and our little children would be left in a lonesome and unhappy situation if I went away. It was mighty hard to go against such arguments as these; but my countrymen had been murdered, and I knew that the next thing would be, that the Indians would be scalping the women and children all about there, if we didn't put a stop to it. I reasoned the case with her as well as I could, and told her, that if every man would wait till his wife got willing for him to go to war, there would be no fighting done, until we would all be killed in our own houses; that I was as able to go as any man in the world; and that I believed it was a duty I owed to my country. Whether she was satisfied with this reasoning or not, she did not tell me; but seeing I was bent on it, all she did was to cry a little, and turn about to her work. The truth is, my dander was up, and nothing but war could bring it right again.

I went to Winchester, where the muster was to be, and a great many people had collected, for there was as much fuss among the people about the war as there is now about moving the deposites. When the men were paraded, a lawyer by the name of Jones addressed us, and closed by turning out himself, and enquiring, at the same time, who among us felt like we could fight Indians? This was the same Mr. Jones who afterwards served in Congress, from the state of Tennessee. He informed us he wished to raise a company, and that then the men should meet and elect their own officers. I believe I was about the second or third man that step'd out; but on marching up and down the regiment a few times, we found we had a large company. We volunteered for sixty days, as it was supposed our services would not be longer wanted. A day or two after this we met and elected Mr. Jones our captain, and also elected our other officers. We then received orders to start on the next Monday week; before which time, I had fixed as well as I could to go, and my wife had equip'd me as well as she was able for the camp. The time arrived; I took a parting farewell of my wife and my little boys, mounted my horse, and set sail, to join my company. Expecting to be gone only a short time, I took no more clothing with me than I supposed would be necessary, so that if I got into an Indian battle, I might not be pestered with any unnecessary plunder, to prevent my having a fair shake with them. We all met and went ahead, till we passed Huntsville, and camped at a large spring called Beaty's spring. Here we staid for several days, in which time the troops began to collect from all quarters. At last we mustered about thirteen hundred strong, all mounted volunteers, and all determined to fight, judging from myself, for I felt wolfish all over. I verily believe the whole army was of the real grit. Our captain didn't want any other sort; and to try them he several times told his men, that if any of them wanted to go back home, they might do so at any time, before they were regularly mustered into the service. But he had the honour to command all his men from first to last, as not one of them left him.

Gen'l. Jackson had not yet left Nashville with his old foot volunteers, that had gone with him to Natchez in 1812, the year before. While we remained at the spring, a Major Gibson came, and wanted some volunteers to go with him across the Tennessee river and into the Creek nation, to find out the movements of the Indians. He came to my captain, and asked for two of his best woods-men, and such as were best with a rifle. The captain pointed me out to him, and said he would be security that I would go as far as the major would himself, or any other man. I willingly engaged to go with him, and asked him to let me choose my own mate to go with me, which he said I might do. I chose a young man by the name of George Russell, a son of old Major Russell, of Tennessee. I called him up, but Major Gibson said he thought he hadn't beard enough to please him,—he wanted men, and not boys. I must confess I was a little nettled at this; for I know'd George Russell, and I know'd there was no mistake in him; and I didn't think that courage ought to be measured by the beard, for fear a goat would have the preference over a man. I told the major he was on the wrong scent; that Russell could go as far as he could, and I must have him along. He saw I was a little wrathy, and said I had the best chance of

 knowing, and agreed that it should be as I wanted it. He told us to be ready early in the morning for a start; and so we were. We took our camp equipage, mounted our horses, and, thirteen in number, including the major, we cut out. We went on, and crossed the Tennessee river at a place called Ditto's Landing; and then traveled about seven miles further, and took up camp for the night. Here a man by the name of John Haynes overtook us. He had been an Indian trader in that part of the nation, and was well acquainted with it. He went with us as a pilot. The next morning, however, Major Gibson and myself concluded we should separate and take different directions to see what discoveries we could make; so he took seven of the men, and I five, making thirteen in all, including myself. He was to go by the house of a Cherokee Indian, named Dick Brown, and I was to go by Dick's father's; and getting all the information we could, we were to meet that evening where the roads came together, fifteen miles the other side of Brown's. At old Mr. Brown's I got a half blood Cherokee to agree to go with me, whose name was Jack Thompson. He was not then ready to start, but was to fix that evening, and overtake us at the fork road where I was to meet Major Gibson. I know'd it wouldn't be safe to camp right at the road; and so I told Jack, that when he got to the fork he must holler like an owl, and I would answer him in the same way; for I know'd it would be night before he got there. I and my men then started, and went on to the place of meeting, but Major Gibson was not there. We waited till almost dark, but still he didn't come. We then left the Indian trace a little distance, and turning into the head of a hollow, we struck up camp. It was about ten o'clock at night, when I heard my owl, and I answered him. Jack soon found us, and we determined to rest there during the night. We staid also next morning till after breakfast: but in vain, for the major didn't still come.

I told the men we had set out to hunt a fight, and I wouldn't go back in that way; that we must go ahead, and see what the red men were at. We started, and went to a Cherokee town about twenty miles off; and after a short stay there, we pushed on to the house of a man by the name of Radcliff. He was a white man, but had married a Creek woman, and lived just in the edge of the Creek nation. He had two sons, large likely fellows, and a great deal of potatoes and corn, and, indeed, almost every thing else to go on; so we fed our horses and got dinner with him, and seemed to be doing mighty well. But he was bad scared all the time. He told us there had been ten painted warriors at his house only an hour before, and if we were discovered there, they would kill us, and his family with us. I replied to him, that my business was to hunt for just such fellows as he had described, and I was determined not to go back until I had done it. Our dinner being over, we saddled up our horses, and made ready to start. But some of my small company I found were disposed to return. I told them, if we were to go back then, we should never hear the last of it; and I was determined to go ahead. I knowed some of them would go with me, and that the rest were afraid to go back by themselves; and so we pushed on to the camp of some of the friendly Creeks, which was distant about eight miles. The moon was about the full, and the night was clear; we therefore had the benefit of her light from night to morning, and I knew if we were placed in such danger as to make a retreat necessary, we could travel by night as well as in the day time.

We had not gone very far, when we met two negroes, well mounted on Indian ponies, and each with a good rifle. They had been taken from their owners by the Indians, and were running away from them, and trying to get back to their masters again. They were brothers, both very large and likely, and could talk Indian as well as English. One of them I sent on to Ditto's Landing, the other I took back with me. It was after dark when we got to the camp, where we found about forty men, women, and children. They had bows and arrows, and I turned in to shooting with their boys by a pine light. In this way we amused ourselves very well for a while; but at last the negro, who had been talking to the Indians, came to me and told me they were very much alarmed, for the "red sticks," as they called the war party of the Creeks, would come and find us there; and, if so, we should all be killed. I directed him to tell them that I would watch, and if one would come that night, I would carry the skin of his head home to make me a mockasin. When he made this communication, the Indians laughed aloud. At about ten o'clock at night we all concluded to try to sleep a little; but that our horses might be ready for use, as the treasurer said of the drafts on the United States' bank, on certain "contingences," we tied them up with our saddles on them, and every thing to our hand, if in the night our quarters should get uncomfortable.

We lay down with our guns in our arms, and I had just gotten into a dose of sleep, when I heard the sharpest scream that ever escaped the throat of a human creature. It was more like a wrathy painter than any thing else. The negro understood it, and he sprang to me; for tho' I heard the noise well enough, yet I wasn't wide awake enough to get up. So the negro caught me, and said the red sticks was coming. I rose quicker then, and asked what was the matter? Our negro had gone and talked with the Indian who had just fetched the scream, as he come into camp, and learned from him, that the war party had been crossing the Coosa river all day at the Ten islands; and were going on to meet Jackson, and this Indian had come as a runner. This news very much alarmed the friendly Indians in camp, and they were all off in a few minutes. I felt bound to make this intelligence known as soon as possible to the army we had left at the landing; and so we all mounted our horses, and put out in a long lope to make our way back to that place. We were about sixty-five miles off. We went on to the same Cherokee town we had visited on our way out, having first called at Radcliff's, who was off with his family; and at the town we found large fires burning, but not a single Indian was to be seen. They were all gone. These circumstances were calculated to lay our dander a little, as it appeared we must be in great danger; though we could easily have licked any force of not more than five to one. But we expected the whole nation would be on us, and against such fearful odds we were not so rampant for a fight.

We therefore staid only a short time in the light of the fires about the town, preferring the light of the moon and the shade of the woods. We pushed on till we got again to old Mr. Brown's, which was still about thirty miles from where we had left the main army. When we got there, the chickens were just at the first crowing for day. We fed our horses, got a morsel to eat ourselves, and again cut out. About ten o'clock in the morning we reached the camp, and I reported to Col. Coffee the news. He didn't seem to mind my report a bit, and this raised my dander higher than ever; but I knowed I had to be on my best behaviour, and so I kept it all to myself; though I was so mad that I was burning inside like a tar-kiln, and I wonder that the smoke hadn't been pouring out of me at all points.

Major Gibson hadn't yet returned, and we all began to think he was killed; and that night they put out a double guard. The next day the major got in, and brought a worse tale than I had, though he stated the same facts, so far as I went. This seemed to put our colonel all in a fidget; and it convinced me, clearly, of one of the hateful ways of the world. When I made my report, it wasn't believed, because I was no officer; I was no great man, but just a poor soldier. But when the same thing was reported by Major Gibson!! why, then, it was all as true as preaching, and the colonel believed it every word.

He, therefore, ordered breastworks to be thrown up, near a quarter of a mile long, and sent an express to Fayetteville, where General Jackson and his troops was, requesting them to push on like the very mischief, for fear we should all be cooked up to a crack-lin before they could get there. Old Hickory-face made a forced march on getting the news; and on the next day, he and his men got into camp, with their feet all blistered from the effects of their swift journey. The volunteers, therefore, stood guard altogether, to let them rest.

CHAPTER VI.

About eight hundred of the volunteers, and of that number I was one, were now sent back, crossing the Tennessee river, and on through Huntsville, so as to cross the river again at another place, and to get on the Indians in another direction. After we passed

Huntsville, we struck on the river at the Muscle Shoals, and at a place on them called Melton's Bluff. This river is here about two miles wide, and a rough bottom; so much so, indeed, in many places, as to be dangerous; and in fording it this time, we left several of the horses belonging to our men, with their feet fast in the crevices of the rocks. The men, whose horses were thus left, went ahead on foot. We pushed on till we got to what was called the Black Warrior's town, which stood near the very spot where Tuscaloosa now stands, which is the seat of government for the state of Alabama.

This Indian town was a large one; but when we arrived we found the Indians had all left it.

There was a large field of corn standing out, and a pretty good supply in some cribs. There was also a fine quantity of dried beans, which were very acceptable to us; and without delay we secured them as well as the corn, and then burned the town to ashes; after which we left the place.

In the field where we gathered the corn we saw plenty of fresh Indian tracks, and we had no doubt they had been scared off by our arrival.

We then went on to meet the main army at the fork road, where I was first to have met Major Gibson. We got that evening as far back as the encampment we had made the night before we reached the Black Warrior's town, which we had just destroyed. The next day we were entirely out of meat. I went to Col. Coffee, who was then in command of us, and asked his leave to hunt as we marched. He gave me leave, but told me to take mighty good care of myself. I turned aside to hunt, and had not gone far when I found a deer that had just been killed and skinned, and his flesh was still warm and smoking. From this I was sure that the Indian who had killed it had been gone only a very few minutes; and though I was never much in favour of one hunter stealing from another, yet meat was so scarce in camp, that I thought I must go in for it. So I just took up the deer on my horse before me, and carried it on till night. I could have sold it for almost any price I would have asked; but this wasn't my rule, neither in peace nor war. Whenever I had any thing, and saw a fellow being suffering, I was more anxious to relieve him than to benefit myself. And this is one of the true secrets of my being a poor man to this day. But it is my way; and while it has often left me with an empty purse, which is as near the devil as any thing else I have seen, yet it has never left my heart empty of consolations which money couldn't buy,—the consolations of having sometimes fed the hungry and covered the naked.

I gave all my deer away, except a small part I kept for myself, and just sufficient to make a good supper for my mess; for meat was getting to be a rarity to us all. We had to live mostly on parched corn. The next day we marched on, and at night took up camp near a large cane brake. While here, I told my mess I would again try for some meat; so I took my rifle and cut out, but hadn't gone far, when I discovered a large gang of hogs. I shot one of them down in his tracks, and the rest broke directly towards the camp. In a few minutes, the guns began to roar, as bad as if the whole army had been in an Indian battle; and the hogs to squeal as bad as the pig did, when the devil turned barber. I shouldered my hog, and went on to the camp; and when I got there I found they had killed a good many of the hogs, and a fine fat cow into the bargain, that had broke out of the cane brake. We did very well that night, and the next morning marched on to a Cherokee town, where our officers stop'd, and gave the inhabitants an order on Uncle Sam for their cow, and the hogs we had killed. The next day we met the main army, having had, as we thought, hard times, and a plenty of them, though we had yet seen hardly the beginning of trouble.

After our meeting we went on to Radcliff's, where I had been before while out as a spy; and when we got there, we found he had hid all his provisions. We also got into the secret, that he was the very rascal who had sent the runner to the Indian camp, with the news that the "red sticks" were crossing at the Ten Islands; and that his object was to scare me and my men away, and send us back with a false alarm.

To make some atonement for this, we took the old scroundrell's two big sons with us, and made them serve in the war.

We then marched to a place, which we called Camp Wills; and here it was that Captain Cannon was promoted to a colonel, and Colonel Coffee to a general. We then marched to the Ten

Islands, on the Coosa river, where we established a fort; and our spy companies were sent out. They soon made prisoners of Bob Catala and his warriors, and, in a few days afterwards, we heard of some Indians in a town about eight miles off. So we mounted our horses, and put out for that town, under the direction of two friendly Creeks we had taken for pilots. We had also a Cherokee colonel, Dick Brown, and some of his men with us. When we got near the town we divided; one of our pilots going with each division. And so we passed on each side of the town, keeping near to it, until our lines met on the far side. We then closed up at both ends, so as to surround it completely; and then we sent Captain Hammond's company of rangers to bring on the affray. He had advanced near the town, when the Indians saw him, and they raised the yell, and came running at him like so many red devils. The main army was now formed in a hollow square around the town, and they pursued Hammond till they came in reach of us. We then gave them a fire, and they returned it, and then ran back into their town. We began to close on the town by making our files closer and closer, and the Indians soon saw they were our property. So most of them wanted us to take them prisoners; and their squaws and all would run and take hold of any of us they could, and give themselves up. I saw seven squaws have hold of one man, which made me think of the Scriptures. So I hollered out the Scriptures was fulfilling; that there was seven women holding to one man's coat tail. But I believe it was a hunting-shirt all the time. We took them all prisoners that came out to us in this way; but I saw some warriors run into a house, until I counted forty-six of them. We pursued them until we got near the house, when we saw a squaw sitting in the door, and she placed her feet against the bow she had in her hand, and then took an arrow, and, raising her feet, she drew with all her might, and let fly at us, and she killed a man, whose name, I believe, was Moore. He was a lieutenant, and his death so enraged us all, that she was fired on, and had at least twenty balls blown through her. This was the first man I ever saw killed with a bow and arrow. We now shot them like dogs; and then set the house on fire, and burned it up with the forty-six warriors in it. I recollect seeing a boy who was shot down near the house. His arm and thigh was broken, and he was so near the burning house that the grease was stewing out of him. In this situation he was still trying to crawl along; but not a murmur escaped him, though he was only about twelve years old. So sullen is the Indian, when his dander is up, that he had sooner die than make a noise, or ask for quarters.

The number that we took prisoners, being added to the number we killed, amounted to one hundred and eighty-six; though I don't remember the exact number of either. We had five of our men killed. We then returned to our camp, at which our fort was erected, and known by the name of Fort Strother. No provisions had yet reached us, and we had now been for several days on half rations. However we went back to our Indian town on the next day, when many of the carcasses of the Indians were still to be seen. They looked very awful, for the burning had not entirely consumed them, but given them a very terrible appearance, at least what remained of them. It was, somehow or other, found out that the house had a potatoe cellar under it, and an immediate examination was made, for we were all as hungry as wolves. We found a fine chance of potatoes in it, and hunger compelled us to eat them, though I had a little rather not, if I could have helped it, for the oil of the Indians we had burned up on the day before had run down on them, and they looked like they had been stewed with fat meat. We then again returned to the army, and remained there for several days almost starving, as all our beef was gone. We commenced eating the beef-hides, and continued to eat every scrap we could lay our hands on. At length an Indian came to our guard one night, and hollered, and said he wanted to see "Captain Jackson." He was conducted to the general's markee, into which he entered, and in a few minutes we received orders to prepare for marching.

In an hour we were all ready, and took up the line of march. We crossed the Coosa river, and went on in the direction to Fort Taladega. When we arrived near the place, we met eleven hundred painted warriors, the very choice of the Creek nation. They had encamped near the fort, and had informed the friendly Indians who were in it, that if they didn't come out, and fight with them against the whites, they would take their fort and all their ammunition and provision. The friendly party asked three days to consider of it, and agreed that if on the third day they didn't come out ready to fight with them, they might take their fort. Thus they put them off. They then immediately started their runner to General Jackson, and he and the army pushed over, as I have just before stated.

The camp of warriors had their spies out, and discovered us coming, some time before we got to the fort. They then went to the friendly Indians, and told them Captain Jackson was coming, and had a great many fine horses, and blankets, and guns, and every thing else; and if they would come out and help to whip him, and to take his plunder, it should all be divided with those in the fort. They promised that when Jackson came, they would then come out and help to whip him. It was about an hour by sun in the morning, when we got near the fort. We were piloted by friendly Indians, and divided as we had done on a former occasion, so as to go to the right and left of the fort, and, consequently, of the warriors who were camped near it. Our lines marched on, as before, till they met in front, and then closed in the rear, forming again into a hollow square. We then sent on old Major Russell, with his spy company, to bring on the battle; Capt. Evans' company went also. When they got near the fort, the top of it was lined with the friendly Indians, crying out as loud as they could roar, "How-dy-do, brother, how-dy-do?" They kept this up till Major Russel had passed by the fort, and was moving on towards the warriors. They were all painted as red as scarlet, and were just as naked as they were born. They had concealed themselves under the bank of a branch, that ran partly around the fort, in the manner of a half moon. Russel was going right into their circle, for he couldn't see them, while the Indians on the top of the fort were trying every plan to show him his danger. But he couldn't understand them. At last, two of them jumped from it, and ran, and took his horse by the bridle, and pointing to where they were, told him there were thousands of them lying under the bank. This brought them to a halt, and about this moment the Indians fired on them, and came rushing forth like a cloud of Egyptian locusts, and screaming like all the young devils had been turned loose, with the old devil of all at their head. Russel's company quit their horses, and took into the fort, and their horses ran up to our line, which was then in full view. The warriors then came yelling on, meeting us, and continued till they were within shot of us, when we fired and killed a considerable number of them. They then broke like a gang of steers, and ran across to our other line, where they were again fired on; and so we kept them running from one line to the other, constantly under a heavy fire, until we had killed upwards of four hundred of them. They fought with guns, and also with their bows and arrows; but at length they made their escape through a part of our line, which was made up of drafted militia, which broke ranks, and they passed. We lost fifteen of our men, as brave fellows as ever lived or died. We buried them all in one grave, and started back to our fort; but before we got there, two more of our men died of wounds they had received; making our total loss seventeen good fellows in that battle.

We now remained at the fort a few days, but no provision came yet, and we were all likely to perish. The weather also began to get very cold; and our clothes were nearly worn out, and horses getting very feeble and poor. Our officers proposed to Gen'l. Jackson to let us return home and get fresh horses, and fresh clothing, so as to be better prepared for another campaign; for our sixty days had long been out, and that was the time we entered for. But the general took "the responsibility" on himself, and refused. We were, however, determined to go, as I am to put back the deposites, if I can. With this, the general issued his orders against it, as he has against the bank. But we began to fix for a start, as provisions were too scarce; just as Clay, and Webster, and myself are preparing to fix bank matters, on account of the scarcity of money. The general went and placed his cannon on a bridge we had to cross, and ordered out his regulars and drafted men to keep us from crossing; just as he has planted his Globe and K. C. to alarm the bank men, while his regulars and militia in Congress are to act as artillery men. But when the militia started to guard the bridge, they would holler back to us to bring their knapsacks along when we come, for they wanted to go as bad as we did; just as many a good fellow now wants his political knapsack brought along, that if, when we come to vote, he sees he has a fair shake to go, he may join in and help us to take back the deposites.

We got ready and moved on till we came near the bridge, where the general's men were all strung along on both sides, just like the office-holders are now, to keep us from getting along to the help of the country and the people. But we all had our flints ready picked, and our guns ready primed, that if we were fired on we might fight our way through, or all die together; just as we are now determined to save the country from ready ruin, or to sink down with it. When we came still nearer the bridge we heard the guards cocking their guns, and we did the same; just as we have had it in Congress, while the "government" regulars and the people's volunteers have all been setting their political triggers. But, after all, we marched boldly on, and not a gun was fired, nor a life lost; just as I hope it will be again, that we shall not be afraid of the general's Globe, nor his K. C., nor his regulars, nor their trigger snapping; but just march boldly over the executive bridge, and take the deposites back where the law placed them, and where they ought to be. When we had passed, no further attempt was made to stop us; but the general said, we were "the damned'st volunteers he had ever seen in his life; that we would volunteer and go out and fight, and then at our pleasure would volunteer and go home again, in spite of the devil." But we went on; and near Huntsville we met a reinforcement who were going on to join the army. It consisted of a regiment of volunteers, and was under the command of some one whose name I can't remember. They were sixty-day volunteers.

We got home pretty safely, and in a short time we had procured fresh horses and a supply of clothing better suited for the season; and then we returned to Fort Deposite, where our officers held a sort of a "national convention" on the subject of a message they had received from General Jackson,—demanding that on our return we should serve out six months. We had already served three months instead of two, which was the time we had volunteered for. On the next morning the officers reported to us the conclusions they had come to; and told us, if any of us felt bound to go on and serve out the six months, we could do so; but that they intended to go back home. I knowed if I went back home I couldn't rest, for I felt it my duty to be out; and when out was, somehow or other, always delighted to be in the very thickest of the danger. A few of us, therefore, determined to push on and join the army.

The number I do not recollect, but it was very small.

When we got out there, I joined Major Russel's company of spies. Before we reached the place, General Jackson had started. We went on likewise, and overtook him at a place where we established a fort, called Fort Williams, and leaving men to guard it, we went ahead; intending to go to a place called the Horse-shoe bend of the Talapoosa river. When we came near that place, we began to find Indian sign plenty, and we struck up camp for the night. About two hours before day, we heard our guard firing, and we were all up in little or no time. We mended up our camp fires, and then fell back in the dark, expecting to see the Indians pouring in; and intending, when they should do so, to shoot them by the light of our own fires. But it happened that they did not rush in as we had expected, but commenced a fire on us as we were. We were encamped in a hollow square, and we not only returned the fire, but continued to shoot as well as we could in the dark, till day broke, when the Indians disappeared. The only guide we had in shooting was to notice the flash of their guns, and then shoot as directly at the place as we could guess.

In this scrape we had four men killed, and several wounded; but whether we killed any of the Indians or not we never could tell, for it is their custom always to carry off their dead, if they can possibly do so. We buried ours, and then made a large log heap over them, and set it on fire, so that the place of their deposite might not be known to the savages, who, we knew, would seek for them, that they might scalp them. We made some horse litters for our wounded, and took up a retreat. We moved on till we came to a large creek which we had to cross; and about half of our men had crossed, when the Indians commenced firing on our left wing, and they kept it up very warmly. We had left Major Russel and his brother at the camp we had moved from that morning, to see what discovery they could make as to the movements of the Indians; and about this time, while a warm fire was kept up on our left, as I have just stated, the major came up in our rear, and was closely pursued by a large number of Indians, who immediately commenced a fire on our artillery men. They hid themselves behind a large log, and could kill one of our men almost every shot, they being in open ground and exposed. The worst of all was, two of our colonels just at this trying moment left their men, and by a forced march, crossed the creek out of the reach of the fire. Their names, at this late day, would do the world no good, and my object is history alone, and not the slightest interference with character. An opportunity was now afforded for Governor Carroll to distinguish himself, and on this occasion he did so, by greater bravery than I ever saw any other man display. In truth, I believe, as firmly as I do that General Jackson is president, that if it hadn't been for Carroll, we should all have been genteely licked that time, for we were in a devil of a fix; part of our men on one side of the creek, and part on the other, and the Indians all the time pouring it on us, as hot as fresh mustard to a sore shin. I will not say exactly that the old general was whip'd; but I will say, that if we escaped it at all, it was like old Henry Snider going to heaven, "mita tam tite squeeze." I think he would confess himself, that he was nearer whip'd this time than he was at any other, for I know that all the world couldn't make him acknowledge that he was pointedly whip'd. I know I was mighty glad when it was over, and the savages quit us, for I had begun to think there was one behind every tree in the woods.

We buried our dead, the number of whom I have also forgotten; and again made horse litters to carry our wounded, and so we put out, and returned to Fort Williams, from which place we had started. In the mean time, my horse had got crippled, and was unfit for service, and as another reinforcement had arrived, I thought they could get along without me for a short time; so I got a furlough and went home, for we had had hard times again on this hunt, and I began to feel as though I had done Indian fighting enough for one time. I remained at home until after the army had returned to the Horse-shoe bend, and fought the battle there. But not being with them at that time, of course no history of that fight can be expected of me.

CHAPTER VII.

Soon after this, an army was to be raised to go to Pensacola, and I determined to go again with them, for I wanted a small taste of British fighting, and I supposed they would be there.

Here again the entreaties of my wife were thrown in the way

of my going, but all in vain; for I always had a way of just going ahead, at whatever I had a mind to. One of my neighbours,
hearing I had determined to go, came to me, and offered me a
hundred dollars to go in his place as a substitute, as he had been
drafted. I told him I was better raised than to hire myself out to be
shot at; but that I would go, and he should go too, and in that way
the government would have the services of us both. But we didn't
call General Jackson "the government" in those days, though we
used to go and fight under him in the war.

I fixed up, and joined old Major Russel again; but we couldn't
start with the main army, but followed on, in a little time, after
them. In a day or two, we had a hundred and thirty men in our
company; and we went over and crossed the Muscle Shoals at
the same place where I had crossed when first out, and when we
burned the Black Warriors' town. We passed through the Choctaw
and Chickesaw nations, on to Fort Stephens, and from thence to
what is called the Cut-off, at the junction of the Tom-Bigby with
the Alabama river. This place is near the old Fort Mimms, where
the Indians committed the great butchery at the commencement
of the war.

We were here about two days behind the main army, who had
left their horses at the Cut-off, and taken it on foot; and they did
this because there was no chance for forage between there and
Pensacola. We did the same, leaving men enough to take care of
our horses, and cut out on foot for that place. It was about eighty
miles off; but in good heart we shouldered our guns, blankets,
and provisions, and trudged merrily on. About twelve o'clock the
second day, we reached the encampment of the main army, which
was situated on a hill, overlooking the city of Pensacola. My com-
mander, Major Russel, was a great favourite with Gen'l. Jackson,
and our arrival was hailed with great applause, though we were
a little after the feast; for they had taken the town and fort before
we got there. That evening we went down into the town, and
could see the British fleet lying in sight of the place. We got some
liquor, and took a "horn" or so, and went back to the camp. We
remained there that night, and in the morning we marched back
towards the Cut-off. We pursued this direction till we reached
old Fort Mimms, where we remained two or three days. It was

here that Major Russel was promoted from his command, which was only that of a captain of spies, to the command of a major in the line. He had been known long before at home as old Major Russel, and so we all continued to call him in the army. A Major Childs, from East Tennessee, also commanded a battalion, and his and the one Russel was now appointed to command, composed a regiment, which, by agreement with General Jackson, was to quit his army and go to the south, to kill up the Indians on the Scamby river.

General Jackson and the main army set out the next morning for New Orleans, and a Colonel Blue took command of the regiment which I have before described. We remained, however, a few days after the general's departure, and then started also on our route. As it gave rise to so much war and bloodshed, it may not be improper here to give a little description of Fort Mimms, and the manner in which the Indian war commenced. The fort was built right in the middle of a large old field, and in it the people had been forted so long and so quietly, that they didn't apprehend any danger at all, and had, therefore, become quite careless. A small negro boy, whose business it was to bring up the calves at milking time, had been out for that purpose, and on coming back, he said he saw a great many Indians. At this the inhabitants took the alarm, and closed their gates and placed out their guards, which they continued for a few days. But finding that no attack was made, they concluded the little negro had lied; and again threw their gates open, and set all their hands out to work their fields. The same boy was out again on the same errand, when, returning in great haste and alarm, he informed them that he had seen the Indians as thick as trees in the woods. He was not believed, but was tucked up to receive a flogging for the supposed lie; and was actually getting badly licked at the very moment when the Indians came in a troop, loaded with rails, with which they stop'd all the port-holes of the fort on one side except the bastion; and then they fell in to cutting down the picketing. Those inside the fort had only the bastion to shoot from, as all the other holes were spiked up; and they shot several of the Indians, while engaged in cutting. But as fast as one would fall, another would seize up the axe and chop away, until they succeeded in cutting down enough

165

of the picketing to admit them to enter. They then began to rush through, and continued until they were all in. They immediately commenced scalping, without regard to age or sex; having forced the inhabitants up to one side of the fort, where they carried on the work of death as a butcher would in a slaughter pen.

The scene was particularly described to me by a young man who was in the fort when it happened, and subsequently went on with us to Pensacola. He said that he saw his father, and mother, his four sisters, and the same number of brothers, all butchered in the most shocking manner, and that he made his escape by running over the heads of the crowd, who were against the fort wall, to the top of the fort, and then jumping off, and taking to the woods. He was closely pursued by several Indians, until he came to a small byo, across which there was a log. He knew the log was hollow on the under side, so he slip'd under the log and hid himself. He said he heard the Indians walk over him several times back and forward. He remained, nevertheless, still till night, when he came out, and finished his escape. The name of this young man has entirely escaped my recollection, though his tale greatly excited my feelings. But to return to my subject. The regiment marched from where Gen'l. Jackson had left us to Fort Montgomery, which was distant from Fort Mimms about a mile and a half, and there we remained for some days.

Here we supplied ourselves pretty well with beef, by killing wild cattle which had formerly belonged to the people who perished in the fort, but had gone wild after their massacre.

When we marched from Fort Montgomery, we went some distance back towards Pensacola; then we turned to the left, and passed through a poor piny country, till we reached the Scamby river, near which we encamped. We had about one thousand men, and as a part of that number, one hundred and eighty-six Chickesaw and Choctaw Indians with us. That evening a boat landed from Pensacola, bringing many articles that were both good and necessary; such as sugar and coffee, and liquors of all kinds. The same evening, the Indians we had along proposed to cross the river, and the officers thinking it might be well for them to do so, consented; and Major Russell went with them, taking sixteen white men, of which number I was one. We camped on the opposite bank that night, and early in the morning we set out. We had not gone far before we came to a place where the whole country was covered with water, and looked like a sea. We didn't stop for this, tho', but just put in like so many spaniels, and waded on, sometimes up to our armpits, until we reached the pine hills, which made our distance through the water about a mile and a half. Here we struck up a fire to warm ourselves, for it was cold, and we were chilled through by being so long in the water. We again moved on, keeping our spies out; two to our left near the bank of the river, two straight before us, and two others on our right. We had gone in this way about six miles up the river, when our spies on the left came to us leaping the brush like so many old bucks, and informed us that they had discovered a camp of Creek Indians, and that we must kill them. Here we paused for a few minutes, and the prophets pow-wowed over their men awhile, and then got out their paint, and painted them, all according to their custom when going into battle. They then brought their paint to old Major Russell, and said to him, that as he was an offi- cer, he must be painted too. He agreed, and they painted him just as they had done themselves. We let the Indians understand that we white men would first fire on the camp, and then fall back, so as to give the Indians a chance to rush in and scalp them. The Chickasaws marched on our left hand, and the Choctaws on our right, and we moved on till we got in hearing of the camp, where the Indians were employed in beating up what they called chainy briar root. On this they mostly subsisted. On a nearer approach we found they were on an island, and that we could not get to them. While we were chatting about this matter, we heard some guns fired, and in a very short time after a keen whoop, which satisfied us, that whereever it was, there was war on a small scale. With that we all broke, like quarter horses, for the firing; and when we got there we found it was our two front spies, who related to us the following story:—As they were moving on, they had met with two Creeks who were out hunting their horses; as they approached each other, there was a large cluster of green bay bushes exactly between them, so that they were within a few feet of meeting before either was discovered. Our spies walked up to them, and speaking in the Shawnee tongue, informed them that

General Jackson was at Pensacola, and they were making their escape, and wanted to know where they could get something to eat. The Creeks told them that nine miles up the Conaker, the river they were then on, there was a large camp of Creeks, and they had cattle and plenty to eat; and further, that their own camp was on an island about a mile off, and just below the mouth of the Conaker. They held their conversation and struck up a fire, and smoked together, and shook hands, and parted. One of the Creeks had a gun, the other had none; and as soon as they had parted, our Choctaws turned round and shot down the one that had the gun, and the other attempted to run off. They snapped several times at him, but the gun still missing fire, they took after him, and overtaking him, one of them struck him over the head with his gun, and followed up his blows till he killed him.

The gun was broken in the combat, and they then fired off the gun of the Creek they had killed, and raised the war-whoop. When we reached them, they had cut off the heads of both the Indians; and each of those Indians with us would walk up to one of the heads, and taking his war club would strike on it. This was done by every one of them; and when they had got done, I took one of their clubs, and walked up as they had done, and struck it on the head also. At this they all gathered round me, and patting me on the shoulder, would call me "Warrior—warrior."

They scalped the heads, and then we moved on a short distance to where we found a trace leading in towards the river. We took this trace and pursued it, till we came to where a Spaniard had been killed and scalped, together with a woman, who we supposed to be his wife, and also four children. I began to feel mighty ticklish along about this time, for I knowed if there was no danger then, there had been; and I felt exactly like there still was. We, however, went on till we struck the river, and then continued down it till we came opposite to the Indian camp, where we found they were still beating their roots.

It was now late in the evening, and they were in a thick cane brake. We had some few friendly Creeks with us, who said they could decoy them. So we all hid behind trees and logs, while the attempt was made. The Indians would not agree that we should fire, but pick'd out some of their best gunners, and placed them near the river. Our Creeks went down to the river's side, and hailed the camp in the Creek language. We heard an answer, and an Indian man started down towards the river, but didn't come in sight. He went back and again commenced beating his roots, and sent a squaw. She came down, and talked with our Creeks until dark came on. They told her they wanted her to bring them a canoe. To which she replied, that their canoe was on our side; that two of their men had gone out to hunt their horses and hadn't yet returned. They were the same two we had killed. The canoe was found, and forty of our picked Indian warriors were crossed over to take the camp. There was at last only one man in it, and he escaped; and they took two squaws, and ten children, but killed none of them, of course.

We had run nearly out of provisions, and Major Russell had determined to go up the Conaker to the camp we had heard of from the Indians we had killed. I was one that he selected to go down the river that night for provisions, with the canoe, to where we had left our regiment. I took with me a man by the name of John Guess, and one of the friendly Creeks, and cut out. It was very dark, and the river was so full that it overflowed the banks and the adjacent low bottoms. This rendered it very difficult to keep the channel, and particularly as the river was very crooked. At about ten o'clock at night we reached the camp, and were to return by morning to Major Russell, with provisions for his trip up the river; but on informing Colonel Blue of this arrangement, he vetoed it as quick as General Jackson did the bank bill; and said, if Major Russell didn't come back the next day, it would be bad times for him. I found we were not to go up the Conaker to the Indian camp, and a man of my company offered to go up in my place to inform Major Russell. I let him go; and they reached the major, as I was told, about sunrise in the morning, who immediately returned with those who were with him to the regiment, and joined us where we crossed the river, as hereafter stated.

The next morning we all fixed up, and marched down the Scamby to a place called Miller's Landing, where we swam our horses across, and sent on two companies down on the side of the bay opposite to Pensacola, where the Indians had fled when the main army first marched to that place. One was the company of Captain William Russell, a son of the old major, and the other was commanded by a Captain Trimble. They went on, and had a little skirmish with the Indians. They killed some, and took all the balance prisoners, though I don't remember the numbers. We again met those companies in a day or two, and sent the prisoners they had taken on to Fort Montgomery, in charge of some of our Indians.

I did hear, that after they left us, the Indians killed and scalped all the prisoners, and I never heard the report contradicted. I cannot positively say it was true, but I think it entirely probable, for it is very much like the Indian character.

CHAPTER VIII.

When we made a move from the point where we met the companies, we set out for Chatahachy, the place for which we had started when we left Fort Montgomery. At the start we had taken only twenty days' rations of flour, and eight days' rations of beef; and it was now thirty-four days before we reached that place. We were, therefore, in extreme suffering for want of something to eat, and exhausted with our exposure and the fatigues of our journey. I remember well, that I had not myself tasted bread but twice in nineteen days. I had bought a pretty good supply of coffee from the boat that had reached us from Pensacola, on the Scamby, and on that we chiefly subsisted. At length, one night our spies came in, and informed us they had found Holm's village on the Chatahachy river; and we made an immediate push for that place. We traveled all night, expecting to get something to eat when we got there. We arrived about sunrise, and near the place prepared for battle. We were all so furious, that even the certainty of a pretty hard fight could not have restrained us. We made a furious charge on the town, but to our great mortification and surprise, there wasn't a human being in it. The Indians had all run off and left it. We burned the town, however; but, melancholy to tell, we found no provision whatever. We then turned about, and went back to the camp we had left the night before, as nearly starved as any set of poor fellows ever were in the world.

We staid there only a little while, when we divided our regiment;

and Major Childs, with his men, went back the way we had come for a considerable distance, and then turned to Baton Rouge, where they joined General Jackson and the main army on their return from Orleans. Major Russell and his men struck for Fort Decatur, on the Talapoosa river. Some of our friendly Indians, who knew the country, went on ahead of us, as we had no trail except the one they made to follow. With them we sent some of our ablest horses and men, to get us some provisions, to prevent us from absolutely starving to death. As the army marched, I hunted every day, and would kill every hawk, bird, and squirrel that I could find. Others did the same; and it was a rule with us, that when we stop'd at night, the hunters would throw all they killed in a pile, and then we would make a general division among all the men. One evening I came in, having killed nothing that day. I had a very sick man in my mess, and I wanted something for him to eat, even if I starved myself. So I went to the fire of a Captain Cowen, who commanded my company after the promotion of Major Russell, and informed him that I was on the hunt of something for a sick man to eat. I knowed the captain was as bad off as the rest of us, but I found him broiling a turkey's gizzard. He said he had divided the turkey out among the sick, that Major Smiley had killed it, and that nothing else had been killed that day. I immediately went to Smiley's fire, where I found him broiling another gizzard. I told him, that it was the first turkey I had ever seen have two gizzards. But so it was, I got nothing for my sick man. And now seeing that every fellow must shift for himself, I determined that in the morning, I would come up missing; so I took my mess and cut out to go ahead of the army. We know'd that nothing more could happen to us if we went than if we staid, for it looked like it was to be starvation any way; we therefore determined to go on the old saying, root hog or die. We passed two camps, at which our men, that had gone on before us, had killed Indians. At one they had killed nine, and at the other three. About daylight we came to a small river, which I thought was the Scamby; but we continued on for three days, killing little or nothing to eat; till, at last, we all began to get nearly ready to give up the ghost, and lie down and die; for we had no prospect of provision, and we knew we couldn't go much further without it.

We came to a large prairie, that was about six miles across it, and in this I saw a trail which I knowed was made by bear, deer, and turkeys. We went on through it till we came to a large creek, and the low grounds were all set over with wild rye, looking as green as a wheat field. We here made a halt, unsaddled our horses, and turned them loose to graze.

One of my companions, a Mr. Vanzant, and myself, then went up the low grounds to hunt. We had gone some distance, finding nothing; when at last, I found a squirrel; which I shot, but he got into a hole in the tree. The game was small, but necessity is not very particular; so I thought I must have him, and I climbed that tree thirty feet high, without a limb, and pulled him out of his hole. I shouldn't relate such small matters, only to show what lengths a hungry man will go to, to get something to eat. I soon killed two other squirrels, and fired at a large hawk. At this a large gang of turkeys rose from the cane brake, and flew across the creek to where my friend was, who had just before crossed it. He soon fired on a large gobler, and I heard it fall. By this time my gun was loaded again, and I saw one sitting on my side of the creek, which had flew over when he fired; so I blazed away, and down I brought him. I gathered him up, and a fine turkey he was. I now began to think we had struck a breeze of luck, and almost forgot our past sufferings, in the prospect of once more having something to eat. I raised the shout, and my comrade came to me, and we went on to our camp with the game we had killed. While we were gone, two of our mess had been out, and each of them had found a bee tree. We turned into cooking some of our game, but we had neither salt nor bread. Just at this moment, on looking down the creek, we saw our men, who had gone on before us for provisions, coming to us. They came up, and measured out to each man a cupfull of flower. With this, we thickened our soup, when our turkey was cooked, and our friends took dinner with us, and then went on.

We now took our tomahawks, and went and cut our bee-trees, out of which we got a fine chance of honey; though we had been starving so long that we feared to eat much at a time, till, like the Irish by hanging, we got used to it again. We rested that night without moving our camp; and the next morning myself and

Vanzant again turned out to hunt. We had not gone far, before I wounded a fine buck very badly; and while pursuing him, I was walking on a large tree that had fallen down, when from the top of it, a large bear broke out and ran off. I had no dogs, and I was sorry enough for it; for of all the hunting I ever did, I have always delighted most in bear hunting. Soon after this, I killed a large buck; and we had just gotten him to camp, when our poor starved army came up. They told us, that to lessen their sufferings as much as possible, Captain William Russell had had his horse led up to be shot for them to eat, just at the moment that they saw our men returning, who had carried on the flour.

We were now about fourteen miles from Fort Decatur, and we gave away all our meat, and honey, and went on with the rest of the army. When we got there, they could give us only one ration of meat, but not a mouthful of bread. I immediately got a canoe, and taking my gun, crossed over the river, and went to the Big Warrior's town. I had a large hat, and I offered an Indian a silver dollar for my hat full of corn. He told me that his corn was all "shuestea," which in English means, it was all gone. But he showed me where an Indian lived, who, he said, had corn. I went to him, and made the same offer. He could talk a little broken English, and said to me, "You got any powder? You got bullet?" I told him I had. He then said, "Me swap my corn, for powder and bullet." I took out about ten bullets, and showed him; and he proposed to give me a hat full of corn for them. I took him up, mighty quick. I then offered to give him ten charges of powder for another hat full of corn. To this he agreed very willingly. So I took off my hunting-shirt, and tied up my corn; and though it had cost me very little of my powder and lead, yet I wouldn't have taken fifty silver dollars for it. I returned to the camp, and the next morning we started for the Hickory Ground, which was thirty miles off. It was here that General Jackson met the Indians, and made peace with the body of the nation.

We got nothing to eat at this place, and we had yet to go forty-nine miles, over a rough and wilderness country, to Fort Williams. Parched corn, and but little even of that, was our daily subsistence. When we reached Fort Williams, we got one ration of pork and one of flour, which was our only hope until we could reach Fort Strother.

The horses were now giving out, and I remember to have seen thirteen good horses left in one day, the saddles and bridles being thrown away. It was thirty-nine miles to Fort Strother, and we had to pass directly by Fort Talladego, where we first had the big Indian battle with the eleven hundred painted warriors. We went through the old battle ground, and it looked like a great gourd patch; the sculls of the Indians who were killed still lay scattered all about, and many of their frames were still perfect, as the bones had not separated. But about five miles before we got to this battle ground, I struck a trail, which I followed until it led me to one of their towns. Here I swap'd some more of my powder and bullets for a little corn.

I pursued on, by myself, till some time after night, when I came up with the rest of the army. That night my company and myself did pretty well, as I divided out my corn among them. The next morning we met the East Tennessee troops, who were on their road to Mobile, and my youngest brother was with them. They had plenty of corn and provisions, and they gave me what I wanted for myself and my horse. I remained with them that night, though my company went across the Coosa river to the fort, where they also had the good fortune to find plenty of provisions. Next morning, I took leave of my brother and all my old neighbours, for there were a good many of them with him, and crossed over to my men at the fort. Here I had enough to go on, and after remaining a few days, cut out for home. Nothing more, worthy of the reader's attention, transpired till I was safely landed at home once more with my wife and children. I found them all well and doing well; and though I was only a rough sort of a backwoodsman, they seemed mighty glad to see me, however little the quality folks might suppose it. For I do reckon we love as hard in the backwood country, as any people in the whole creation.

But I had been home only a few days, when we received orders to start again, and go on to the Black Warrior and Cahawba rivers, to see if there was no Indians there. I know'd well enough there was none, and I wasn't willing to trust my craw any more where there was neither any fighting to do, nor any thing to go on; and so I agreed to give a young man, who wanted to go, the balance of my wages if he would serve out my time, which was about a month. He did so, and when they returned, sure enough they hadn't seen an Indian any more than if they had been all the time chopping wood in my clearing. This closed my career as a warrior, and I am glad of it, for I like life now a heap better than I did then; and I am glad all over that I lived to see these times, which I should not have done if I had kept fooling along in war, and got used up at it. When I say I am glad, I just mean I am glad I am alive, for there is a confounded heap of things I an't glad of at all. I an't glad, for example, that the "government" moved the deposites, and if my military glory should take such a turn as to make me president after the general's time, I'll move them back; yes, I, the "government," will "take the responsibility," and move them back again. If I don't, I wish I may be shot.

But I am glad that I am now through war matters, and I reckon the reader is too, for they have no fun in them at all; and less if he had had to pass through them first, and then to write them afterwards. But for the dullness of their narrative, I must try to make amends by relating some of the curious things that happened to me in private life, and when forced to become a public man, as I shall have to be again, if ever I consent to take the presidential chair.

CHAPTER IX.

I continued at home now, working my farm for two years, as the war finally closed soon after I quit the service. The battle at New Orleans had already been fought, and treaties were made with the Indians which put a stop to their hostilities.

But in this time, I met with the hardest trial which ever falls to the lot of man. Death, that cruel leveller of all distinctions,—to whom the prayers and tears of husbands, and of even helpless infancy, are addressed in vain,—entered my humble cottage, and tore from my children an affectionate good mother, and from me a tender and loving wife.

It is a scene long gone by, and one which it would be supposed I had almost forgotten; yet when I turn my memory back on it, it seems as but the work of yesterday. It was the doing of the Almighty, whose ways are always right, though we sometimes think they fall heavily on us; and as painful as is even yet the remembrance of her sufferings, and the loss sustained by my little children and myself, yet I have no wish to lift up the voice of complaint. I was left with three children; the two oldest were sons, the youngest a daughter, and, at that time, a mere infant. It appeared to me, at that moment, that my situation was the worst in the world. I couldn't bear the thought of scattering my children, and so I got my youngest brother, who was also married, and his family to live with me. They took as good care of my children as they well could, but yet it wasn't all like the care of a mother. And though their company was to me in every respect like that of a brother and sister, yet it fell far short of being like that of a wife. So I came to the conclusion it wouldn't do, but that I must have another wife.

There lived in the neighbourhood, a widow lady whose husband had been killed in the war. She had two children, a son and daughter, and both quite small, like my own. I began to think, that as we were both in the same situation, it might be that we could do something for each other; and I therefore began to hint a little around the matter, as we were once and a while together. She was a good industrious woman, and owned a snug little farm, and lived quite comfortable. I soon began to pay my respects to her in real good earnest; but I was as sly about it as a fox when he is going to rob a hen-roost. I found that my company wasn't at all disagreeable to her; and I thought I could treat her children with so much friendship as to make her a good stepmother to mine, and in this I wan't mistaken, as we soon bargained, and got married, and then went ahead. In a great deal of peace we raised our first crop of children, and they are all married and doing well. But we had a second crop together; and I shall notice them as I go along, as my wife and myself both had a hand in them, and they therefore belong to the history of my second marriage.

The next fall after this marriage, three of my neighbours and myself determined to explore a new country. Their names were Robinson, Frazier, and Rich. We set out for the Creek country, crossing the Tennessee river; and after having made a day's travel, we stop'd at the house of one of my old acquaintances, who had settled there after the war. Resting here a day, Frazier turned out to

hunt, being a great hunter; but he got badly bit by a very poison-
ous snake, and so we left him and went on. We passed through a
large rich valley, called Jones's valley, where several other families
had settled, and continued our course till we came near to the
place where Tuscaloosa now stands. Here we camped, as there
were no inhabitants, and hobbled out our horses for the night.
About two hours before day, we heard the bells on our horses going back the way we had come, as they had started to leave us. As
soon as it was daylight, I started in pursuit of them on foot, and
carrying my rifle, which was a very heavy one. I went ahead the
whole day, wading creeks and swamps, and climbing mountains;
but I couldn't overtake our horses, though I could hear of them
at every house they passed. I at last found I couldn't catch up
with them, and so I gave up the hunt, and turned back to the last
house I had passed, and staid there till morning. From the best
calculation we could make, I had walked over fifty miles that day;
and the next morning I was so sore, and fatigued, that I felt like I
couldn't walk any more. But I was anxious to get back to where
I had left my company, and so I started and went on, but mighty
slowly, till after the middle of the day. I now began to feel mighty
sick, and had a dreadful head-ache. My rifle was so heavy, and I
felt so weak, that I lay down by the side of the trace, in a perfect
wilderness too, to see if I wouldn't get better.

 In a short time some Indians came along. They had some ripe
melons, and wanted me to eat some, but I was so sick I couldn't.
They then signed to me, that I would die, and be buried; a thing
I was confoundedly afraid of myself. But I asked them how near
it was to any house? By their signs, again, they made me understand it was a mile and a half. I got up to go; but when I rose, I
reeled about like a cow with the blind staggers, or a fellow who
had taken too many "horns." One of the Indians proposed to go
with me, and carry my gun. I gave him half a dollar, and accepted his offer. We got to the house, by which time I was pretty far
gone, but was kindly received, and got on to a bed. The woman
did all she could for me with her warm teas, but I still continued
bad enough, with a high fever, and generally out of my senses.
The next day two of my neighbours were passing the road, and
heard of my situation, and came to where I was. They were going

nearly the route I had intended to go, to look at the country; and so they took me first on one of their horses, and then on the other, till they got me back to where I had left my company. I expected I would get better, and be able to go on with them, but, instead of this, I got worse and worse; and when we got there, I wan't able to sit up at all. I thought now the jig was mighty nigh up with me, but I determined to keep a stiff upper lip. They carried me to a house, and each of my comrades bought him a horse, and they all set out together, leaving me behind. I knew but little that was going on for about two weeks; but the family treated me with every possible kindness in their power, and I shall always feel thankful to them. The man's name was Jesse Jones. At the end of two weeks I began to mend without the help of a doctor, or of any doctor's means. In this time, however, as they told me, I was speechless for five days, and they had no thought that I would ever speak again,—in Congress or any where else. And so the woman, who had a bottle of Batesman's draps, thought if they killed me, I would only die any how, and so she would try it with me. She gave me the whole bottle, which throwed me into a sweat that continued on me all night; when at last I seemed to make up, and spoke, and asked her for a drink of water. This almost alarmed her, for she was looking every minute for me to die. She gave me the water, and, from that time, I began slowly to mend, and so kept on till I was able at last to walk about a little. I might easily have been mistaken for one of the Kitchen Cabinet, I looked so much like a ghost. I have been particular in giving a history of this sickness, not because I believe it will interest any body much now, nor, indeed, do I certainly know that it ever will. But if I should be forced to take the "white house," then it will be good history; and every one will look on it as important. And I can't, for my life, help laughing now, to think, that when all my folks get around me, wanting good fat offices, how so many of them will say, "What a good thing it was that that kind woman had the bottle of draps, that saved President Crockett's life,—the second greatest and best"!!!!! Good, says I, my noble fellow! You take the post office; or the navy; or the war office; or may-be the treasury. But if I give him the treasury, there's no devil if I don't make him agree first to fetch back them deposites. And if it's even the post office, I'll make him promise to keep his money 'counts without any figuring, as that throws the whole concern heels over head in debt, in little or no time.

But when I got so I could travel a little, I got a waggoner who was passing along to hawl me to where he lived, which was about twenty miles from my house. I still mended as we went along and when we got to his stopping place, I hired one of his horses, and went on home. I was so pale, and so much reduced, that my face looked like it had been half soled with brown paper.

When I got there, it was to the utter astonishment of my wife; for she supposed I was dead. My neighbours who had started with me had returned and took my horse home, which they had found with their's; and they reported that they had seen men who had helped to bury me; and who saw me draw my last breath. I know'd this was a whapper of a lie, as soon as I heard it. My wife had hired a man, and sent him out to see what had become of my money and other things; but I had missed the man as I went in, and he didn't return until some time after I got home, as he went all the way to where I lay sick, before he heard that I was still in the land of the living and a-kicking.

The place on which I lived was sickly, and I was determined to leave it. I therefore set out the next fall to look at the country which had been purchased of the Chickasaw tribe of Indians. I went on to a place called Shoal Creek, about eighty miles from where I lived, and here again I got sick. I took the ague and fever, which I supposed was brought on me by camping out. I remained here for some time, as I was unable to go farther; and in that time, I became so well pleased with the country about there, that I resolved to settle in it. It was just only a little distance in the purchase, and no order had been established there; but I thought I could get along without order as well as any body else. And so I moved and settled myself down on the head of Shoal Creek.

We remained here some two or three years, without any law at all; and so many bad characters began to flock in upon us, that we found it necessary to set up a sort of temporary government of our own. I don't mean that we made any president, and called him the "government," but we met and made what we called a corporation; and I reckon we called it wrong, for it wa'n't a bank,

and hadn't any deposites; and now they call the bank a corporation. But be this as it may, we lived in the back-woods, and didn't
profess to know much, and no doubt used many wrong words.
But we met, and appointed magistrates and constables to keep
order. We didn't fix any laws for them, tho'; for we supposed they
would know law enough, whoever they might be; and so we left
it to themselves to fix the laws.

I was appointed one of the magistrates; and when a man owed a
debt, and wouldn't pay it, I and my constable ordered our warrant, and then he would take the man, and bring him before me
for trial. I would give judgment against him, and then an order
of an execution would easily scare the debt out of him. If any one
was charged with marking his neighbour's hogs, or with stealing
any thing, which happened pretty often in those days,—I would
have him taken, and if there was tolerable grounds for the charge,
I would have him well whip'd and cleared. We kept this up till
our Legislature added us to the white settlements in Giles county; and appointed magistrates by law, to organize matters in the
parts where I lived. They appointed nearly every man a magis-
trate who had belonged to our corporation. I was then, of course,
made a squire according to law; though now the honour rested
more heavily on me than before. For, at first, whenever I told my
constable, says I—"Catch that fellow, and bring him up for trial"—away he went, and the fellow must come, dead or alive; for
we considered this a good warrant, though it was only in verbal
writings. But after I was appointed by the assembly, they told me,
my warrants must be in real writing, and signed; and that I must
keep a book, and write my proceedings in it.

This was a hard business on me, for I could just barely write my
own name; but to do this, and write the warrants too, was at least
a huckleberry over my persimmon. I had a pretty well informed
constable, however; and he aided me very much in this business.
Indeed I had so much confidence in him, that I told him, when
we should happen to be out anywhere, and see that a warrant
was necessary, and would have a good effect, he need'nt take the
trouble to come all the way to me to get one, but he could just fill
out one; and then on the trial I could correct the whole business if
he had committed any error. In this way I got on pretty well, till

by care and attention I improved my handwriting in such manner as to be able to prepare my warrants, and keep my record book, without much difficulty. My judgments were never appealed from, and if they had been they would have stuck like wax, as I gave my decisions on the principles of common justice and honesty between man and man, and relied on natural born sense, and not on law, learning to guide me; for I had never read a page in a law book in all my life.

CHAPTER X.

About the time we were getting under good headway in our new government, a Capt. Matthews came to me and told me he was a candidate for the office of colonel of a regiment, and that I must run for first major in the same regiment. I objected to this, telling him that I thought I had done my share of fighting, and that I wanted nothing to do with military appointments.

He still insisted, until at last I agreed, and of course had every reason to calculate on his support in my election. He was an early settler in that country, and made rather more corn than the rest of us; and knowing it would afford him a good opportunity to electioneer a little, he made a great corn husking, and a great frolic, and gave a general treat, asking every body over the whole country. Myself and my family were, of course, invited. When I got there, I found a very large collection of people, and some friend of mine soon informed me that the captain's son was going to offer against me for the office of major, which he had seemed so anxious for me to get. I cared nothing about the office, but it put my dander up high enough to see, that after he had pressed me so hard to offer, he was countenancing, if not encouraging, a secret plan to beat me. I took the old gentleman out, and asked him about it. He told me it was true his son was going to run as a candidate, and that he hated worse to run against me than any man in the county. I told him his son need give himself no uneasiness about that; that I shouldn't run against him for major, but against his daddy for colonel. He took me by the hand, and we went into the company. He then made a speech, and informed the people that I was his opponent. I mounted up for a speech too. I told the people the cause of my opposing him, remarking that as I had the whole family to run against any way, I was determined to levy on the head of the mess. When the time for the election came, his son was opposed by another man for major; and he and his daddy were both badly beaten. I just now began to take a rise, as in a little time I was asked to offer for the Legislature in the counties of Lawrence and Heckman.

I offered my name in the month of February, and started about the first of March with a drove of horses to the lower part of the state of North Carolina. This was in the year 1821, and I was gone upwards of three months. I returned, and set out electioneering, which was a bran-fire new business to me. It now became necessary that I should tell the people something about the government, and an eternal sight of other things that I knowed nothing more about than I did about Latin, and law, and such things as that. I have said before that in those days none of us called Gen'l. Jackson the government, nor did he seem in as fair a way to become so as I do now; but I knowed so little about it, that if any one had told me he was "the government," I should have believed it, for I had never read even a newspaper in my life, or any thing else, on the subject. But over all my difficulties, it seems to me I was born for luck, though it would be hard for any one to guess what sort. I will, however, explain that hereafter.

I went first into Heckman county, to see what I could do among the people as a candidate. Here they told me that they wanted to move their town nearer to the centre of the county, and I must come out in favour of it. There's no devil if I knowed what this meant, or how the town was to be moved; and so I kept dark, going on the identical same plan that I now find is called "non-committal."

About this time there was a great squirrel hunt on Duck river, which was among my people. They were to hunt two days: then to meet and count the scalps, and have a big barbecue, and what might be called a tip-top country frolic. The dinner, and a general treat, was all to be paid for by the party having taken the fewest scalps. I joined one side, taking the place of one of the hunters, and got a gun ready for the hunt. I killed a great many squirrels, and when we counted scalps, my party was victorious.

The company had every thing to eat and drink that could be furnished in so new a country, and much fun and good humour prevailed. But before the regular frolic commenced, I mean the dancing, I was called on to make a speech as a candidate; which was a business I was as ignorant of as an outlandish negro.
A public document I had never seen, nor did I know there were such things; and how to begin I couldn't tell. I made many apologies, and tried to get off, for I know'd I had a man to run against who could speak prime, and I know'd, too, that I wa'n't able to shuffle and cut with him. He was there, and knowing my ignorance as well as I did myself, he also urged me to make a speech. The truth is, he thought my being a candidate was a mere matter of sport; and didn't think, for a moment, that he was in any danger from an ignorant back-woods bear hunter. But I found I couldn't get off, and so I determined just to go ahead, and leave it to chance what I should say. I got up and told the people, I reckoned they know'd what I come for, but if not, I could tell them. I had come for their votes, and if they didn't watch mighty close, I'd get them too. But the worst of all was, that I couldn't tell them any thing about government. I tried to speak about something, and I cared very little what, until I choked up as bad as if my mouth had been jam'd and cram'd chock full of dry mush. There the people stood, listening all the while, with their eyes, mouths and ear all open, to catch every word I would speak.
At last I told them I was like a fellow I had heard of not long before. He was beating on the head of an empty barrel near the road-side, when a traveler, who was passing along, asked him what he was doing that for? The fellow replied, that there was some cider in that barrel a few days before, and he was trying to see if there was any then, but if there was he couldn't get at it. I told them that there had been a little bit of a speech in me a while ago, but I believed I couldn't get it out.
They all roared out in a mighty laugh, and I told some other anecdotes, equally amusing to them, and believing I had them in a first-rate way, I quit and got down, thanking the people for their attention. But I took care to remark that I was as dry as a powder horn, and that I thought it was time for us all to wet our whistles a little; and so I put off to the liquor stand, and was followed by

the greater part of the crowd.

I felt certain this was necessary, for I knowed my competitor could open government matters to them as easy as he pleased. He had, however, mighty few left to hear him, as I continued with the crowd, now and then taking a horn, and telling good humoured stories, till he was done speaking. I found I was good for the votes at the hunt, and when we broke up, I went on to the town of Vernon, which was the same they wanted me to move. Here they pressed me again on the subject, and I found I could get either party by agreeing with them. But I told them I didn't know whether it would be right or not, and so couldn't promise either way.

Their court commenced on the next Monday, as the barbacue was on a Saturday, and the candidates for governor and for Congress, as well as my competitor and myself, all attended. The thought of having to make a speech made my knees feel mighty weak, and set my heart to fluttering almost as bad as my first love scrape with the Quaker's niece. But as good luck would have it, these big candidates spoke nearly all day, and when they quit, the people were worn out with fatigue, which afforded me a good apology for not discussing the government. But I listened mighty close to them, and was learning pretty fast about political matters. When they were all done, I got up and told some laughable story, and quit. I found I was safe in those parts, and so I went home, and didn't go back again till after the election was over. But to cut this matter short, I was elected, doubling my competitor, and nine votes over.

A short time after this, I was in Pulaski, where I met with Colonel Polk, now a member of Congress from Tennessee. He was at that time a member elected to the Legislature, as well as myself; and in a large company he said to me, "Well, colonel, I suppose we shall have a radical change of the judiciary at the next session of the Legislature." "Very likely, sir," says I, and I put out quicker, for I was afraid some one would ask me what the judiciary was; and if I knowed I wish I may be shot. I don't indeed believe I had ever before heard that there was any such thing in all nature; but still I was not willing that the people there should know how ignorant I was about it.

When the time for meeting of the Legislature arrived, I went on, and before I had been there long, I could have told what the judiciary was, and what the government was too; and many other things that I had known nothing about before.

About this time I met with a very severe misfortune, which I may be pardoned for naming, as it made a great change in my circumstances, and kept me back very much in the world. I had built an extensive grist mill, and powder mill, all connected together, and also a large distillery. They had cost me upwards of three thousand dollars, more than I was worth in the world. The first news that I heard after I got to the Legislature, was, that my mills were—not blown up sky high, as you would guess, by my powder establishment,—but swept away all to smash by a large fresh, that came soon after I left home. I had, of course, to stop my distillery, as my grinding was broken up; and, indeed, I may say, that the misfortune just made a complete mash of me. I had some likely negroes, and a good stock of almost every thing about me, and, best of all, I had an honest wife. She didn't advise me, as is too fashionable, to smuggle up this, and that, and t'other, to go on at home; but she told me, says she, "Just pay up, as long as you have a bit's worth in the world; and then every body will be satisfied, and we will scuffle for more." This was just such talk as I wanted to hear, for a man's wife can hold him devlish uneasy, if she begins to scold, and fret, and perplex him, at a time when he has a full load for a rail-road car on his mind already.

And so, you see, I determined not to break full handed, but thought it better to keep a good conscience with an empty purse, than to get a bad opinion of myself, with a full one. I therefore gave up all I had, and took a bran-fire new start.

CHAPTER XI.

Having returned from the Legislature, I determined to make another move, and so I took my eldest son with me, and a young man by the name of Abram Henry, and cut out for the Obion. I selected a spot when I got there, where I determined to settle; and the nearest house to it was seven miles, the next nearest was fifteen, and so on to twenty. It was a complete wilderness, and full of Indians who were hunting. Game was plenty of almost every kind, which suited me exactly, as I was always fond of hunting. The house which was nearest me, and which, as I have already stated, was seven miles off, and on the different side of the Obion river, belonged to a man by the name of Owens; and I started to go there. I had taken one horse along, to pack our provision, and when I got to the water I hobbled him out to graze, until I got back; as there was no boat to cross the river in, and it was so high that it had overflowed all the bottoms and low country near it. We now took water like so many beavers, notwithstanding it was mighty cold, and waded on. The water would sometimes be up to our necks, and at others not so deep; but I went, of course, before, and carried a pole, with which I would feel along before me, to see how deep it was, and to guard against falling into a slough, as there was many in our way. When I would come to one, I would take out my tomahawk and cut a small tree across it, and then go ahead again. Frequently my little son would have to swim, even where myself and the young man could wade; but we worked on till at last we got to the channel of the river, which made it about half a mile we had waded from where we took water. I saw a large tree that had fallen into the river from the other side, but it didn't reach across. One stood on the same bank where we were, that I thought I could fall, so as to reach the other; and so at it we went with my tomahawk, cutting away till we got it down; and, as good luck would have it, it fell right, and made us a way that we could pass.

When we got over this, it was still a sea of water as far as our eyes could reach. We took into it again, and went ahead, for about a mile, hardly ever seeing a single spot of land, and sometimes very deep. At last we come in sight of land, which was a very pleasing thing; and when we got out, we went but a little way, before we came in sight of the house, which was more pleasing than ever; for we were wet all over, and mighty cold. I felt mighty sorry when I would look at my little boy, and see him shaking like he had the worst sort of an ague, for there was no time for fever then. As we got near to the house, we saw Mr. Owens and several men that were with him, just starting away. They saw us, and stop'd, but looked much astonished until we got up to them, and I made myself known. The men who were with him were the owners of a boat which was the first that ever went that far up the Obion river; and some hands he had hired to carry it about a hundred miles still further up, by water, tho' it was only about thirty by land, as the river is very crooked.

They all turned back to the house with me, where I found Mrs. Owens, a fine, friendly old woman; and her kindness to my little boy did me ten times as much good as any thing she could have done for me, if she had tried her best. The old gentleman set out his bottle to us, and I concluded that if a horn wasn't good then, there was no use for its invention. So I swig'd off about a half pint, and the young man was by no means bashful in such a case; he took a strong pull at it too. I then gave my boy some, and in a little time we felt pretty well. We dried ourselves by the fire, and were asked to go on board of the boat that evening. I agreed to do so, but left my son with the old lady, and myself and my young man went to the boat with Mr. Owens and the others. The boat was loaded with whiskey, flour, sugar, coffee, salt, castings, and other articles suitable for the country; and they were to receive five hundred dollars to land the load at M'Lemore's Bluff, beside the profit they could make on their load. This was merely to show that boats could get up to that point. We staid all night with them, and had a high night of it, as I took steam enough to drive out all the cold that was in me, and about three times as much more. In the morning we concluded to go on with the boat to where a great harricane had crossed the river, and blowed all the timber down into it. When we got there, we found the river was falling fast, and concluded we couldn't get through the timber without more rise; so we drop'd down opposite Mr. Owens' again, where they determined to wait for more water.

The next day it rained rip-roriously, and the river rose pretty considerable, but not enough yet. And so I got the boatsmen all to go out with me to where I was going to settle, and we slap'd up a cabin in little or no time. I got from the boat four barrels of meal, and one of salt, and about ten gallons of whiskey.

To pay for these, I agreed to go with the boat up the river to their landing place. I got also a large middling of bacon, and killed a fine deer, and left them for my young man and my little boy, who were to stay at my cabin till I got back; which I expected would be in six or seven days. We cut out, and moved up to the harricane, where we stop'd for the night. In the morning I started about daylight, intending to kill a deer, as I had no thought they would get the boat through the timber that day. I had gone but a little way before I killed a fine buck, and started to go back to the boat; but on the way I came on the tracks of a large gang of elks, and so I took after them. I had followed them only a little distance when I saw them, and directly after I saw two large bucks. I shot one down, and the other wouldn't leave him; so I loaded my gun, and shot him down too. I hung them up, and went ahead again after my elks. I pursued on till after the middle of the day before I saw them again; but they took the hint before I got in shooting distance, and run off. I still pushed on till late in the evening, when I found I was about four miles from where I had left the boat, and as hungry as a wolf, for I hadn't eaten a bite that day.

I started down the edge of the river low grounds, giving out the pursuit of my elks, and hadn't gone hardly any distance at all, before I saw two more bucks, very large fellows too. I took a blizzard at one of them, and up he tumbled. The other ran off a few jumps and stop'd; and stood there till I loaded again, and fired at him. I knock'd his trotters from under him, and then I hung them both up. I pushed on again; and about sunset I saw three other bucks. I down'd with one of them, and the other two ran off. I hung this one up also, having now killed six that day. I then pushed on till I got to the harricane, and at the lower edge of it, about where I expected the boat was. Here I hollered as hard as I could roar, but could get no answer. I fired off my gun, and the men on the boat fired one too; but quite contrary to my expectation, they had got through the timber, and were about two miles above me. It was now dark, and I had to crawl through the fallen timber the best way I could; and if the reader don't know it was bad enough, I am sure I do. For the vines and briers had grown all through it, and so thick, that a good fat coon couldn't much more than get along. I got through at last, and went on near to where I had killed my last deer, and once more fired off my gun, which was again answered from the boat, which was still a little above me. I moved on as fast as I could, but soon came to water, and not knowing how deep it was, I halted and hollered till they came to me with a skiff. I now got to the boat, without further difficulty; but the briers had worked on me at such a rate, that I felt like I wanted sewing up, all over. I took a pretty stiff horn, which soon made me feel much better; but I was so tired that I could hardly work my jaws to eat.

In the morning, myself and a young man started and brought in the first buck I had killed; and after breakfast we went and brought in the last one. The boat then started, but we again went and got the two I had killed just as I turned down the river in the evening; and we then pushed on and o'ertook the boat, leaving the other two hanging in the woods, as we had now as much as we wanted.

We got up the river very well, but quite slowly; and we landed, on the eleventh day, at the place the load was to be delivered at. They here gave me their skiff, and myself and a young man by the name of Flavius Harris, who had determined to go and live with me, cut out down the river for my cabin, which we reached safely enough.

We turned in and cleared a field, and planted our corn; but it was so late in the spring, we had no time to make rails, and therefore we put no fence around our field. There was no stock, however, nor any thing else to disturb our corn, except the wild varments, and the old serpent himself, with a fence to help him, couldn't keep them out. I made corn enough to do me, and during that spring I killed ten bears, and a great abundance of deer. But in all this time, we saw the face of no white person in that country, except Mr. Owens' family, and a very few passengers, who went out there, looking at the country. Indians, though, were still plenty enough. Having laid by my crap, I went home, which was a distance of about a hundred and fifty miles; and when I got there, I was met by an order to attend a call-session of our Legislature. I attended it, and served out my time, and then returned, and took my family and what little plunder I had, and moved to where I had built my cabin, and made my crap.

I gathered my corn, and then set out for my Fall's hunt. This was in the last of October, 1822. I found bear very plenty, and, indeed, all sorts of game and wild varments, except buffalo. There was none of them. I hunted on till Christmas, having supplied my family very well all along with wild meat, at which time my powder gave out; and I had none either to fire Christmas guns, which is very common in that country, or to hunt with. I had a brother-in-law who had now moved out and settled about six miles west of me, on the opposite side of Rutherford's fork of the Obion river, and he had brought me a keg of powder, but I had never gotten it home. There had just been another of Noah's freshes, and the low grounds were flooded all over with water. I know'd the stream was at least a mile wide which I would have to cross, as the water was from hill to hill, and yet I determined to go on over in some way or other, so as to get my powder. I told this to my wife, and she immediately opposed it with all her might. I still insisted, telling her we had no powder for Christmas, and, worse than all, we were out of meat. She said, we had as well starve as for me to freeze to death or to get drowned, and one or the other was certain if I attempted to go.

But I didn't believe the half of this; and so I took my woolen wrappers, and a pair of mockasins, and put them on, and tied up some dry clothes and a pair of shoes and stockings, and started. But I didn't before know how much any body could suffer and not die. This, and some of my other experiments in water, learned me something about it, and I therefore relate them.

The snow was about four inches deep when I started; and when I got to the water, which was only about a quarter of a mile off, it look'd like an ocean. I put in, and waded on till I come to the channel, where I crossed that on a high log. I then took water again, having my gun and all my hunting tools along, and waded till I came to a deep slough, that was wider than the river itself. I had crossed it often on a log; but, behold, when I got there, no log was to be seen. I knowed of an island in the slough, and a sapling stood on it close to the side of that log, which was now entirely under water. I knowed further, that the water was about eight or ten feet deep under the log, and I judged it to be about three feet deep over it. After studying a little what I should do, I determined to cut a forked sapling, which stood near me, so as to lodge it against the one that stood on the island, in which I succeeded very well. I then cut me a pole, and crawled along on my sapling till I got to the one it was lodged against, which was about six feet above the water. I then felt about with my pole till I found the log, which was just about as deep under the water as I had judged. I then crawled back and got my gun, which I had left at the stump of the sapling I had cut, and again made my way to the place of lodgement, and then climb'd down the other sapling so as to get on the log. I then felt my way along with my feet, in the water, about waist deep, but it was a mighty ticklish business. However, I got over, and by this time I had very little feeling in my feet and legs, as I had been all the time in the water, except what time I was crossing the high log over the river, and climbing my lodged sapling.

I went but a short distance before I came to another slough, over which there was a log, but it was floating on the water. I thought I could walk it, and so I mounted on it; but when I had got about the middle of the deep water, somehow or somehow else, it turned over, and in I went up to my head I waded out of this deep water, and went ahead till I came to the high-land, where I stop'd to pull off my wet clothes, and put on the others, which I had held up with my gun, above the water, when I fell in. I got them on, but my flesh had no feeling in it, I was so cold. I tied up the wet ones, and hung them up in a bush. I now thought I would run, so as to warm myself a little, but I couldn't raise a trot for some time; indeed, I couldn't step more than half the length of my foot. After a while I got better, and went on five miles to the house of my brother-in-law, having not even smelt fire from the time I started. I got there late in the evening, and he was much astonished at seeing me at such a time. I staid all night, and the next morning was most piercing cold, and so they persuaded me not to go home that day. I agreed, and turned out and killed him two deer; but the weather still got worse and colder, instead of better. I staid that night, and in the morning they still insisted I couldn't get home. I knowed the water would be frozen over, but not hard enough to bear me, and so I agreed to stay that day. I went out hunting again, and pursued a big he-bear all day, but didn't kill him. The next morning was bitter cold, but I knowed my family was without meat, and I determined to get home to them, or die a-trying. I took my keg of powder, and all my hunting tools, and cut out.

When I got to the water, it was a sheet of ice as far as I could see. I put on to it, but hadn't got far before it broke through with me; and so I took out my tomahawk, and broke my way along before me for a considerable distance. At last I got to where the ice would bear me for a short distance, and I mounted on it, and went ahead; but it soon broke in again, and I had to wade on till I came to my floating log. I found it so tight this time, that I know'd it couldn't give me another fall, as it was frozen in with the ice. I crossed over it without much difficulty, and worked along till I got to my lodged sapling, and my log under the water. The swiftness of the current prevented the water from freezing over it, and so I had to wade, just as I did when I crossed it before. When I got to my sapling, I left my gun and climbed out with my powder keg first, and then went back and got my gun. By this time I was nearly frozen to death, but I saw all along before me, where the ice had been fresh broke, and I thought it must be a bear straggling about in the water. I, therefore, fresh primed my gun, and, cold as I was, I was determined to make war on him, if we met. But I followed the trail till it led me home, and I then found it had been made by my young man that lived with me, who had been sent by my distressed wife to see, if he could, what had become of me, for they all believed that I was dead. When I got home I was'nt quite dead, but mighty nigh it; but I had my powder, and that was what I went for.

CHAPTER XII.
That night there fell a heavy rain, and it turned to a sleet. In the morning all hands turned out hunting. My young man, and a brother-in-law who had lately settled close by me, went down the river to hunt for turkeys; but I was for larger game. I told them, I had dreamed the night before of having a hard fight with a big black nigger, and I knowed it was a sign that I was to have a battle with a bear; for in a bear country, I never know'd such a dream to fail. So I started to go up above the harricane, determined to have a bear. I had two pretty good dogs, and an old hound, all of which I took along. I had gone about six miles up the river, and it was then about four miles across to the main Obion; so I deter-

mined to strike across to that, as I had found nothing yet to kill. I got on to the river, and turned down it; but the sleet was still getting worse and worse. The bushes were all bent down, and locked together with ice, so that it was almost impossible to get along. In a little time my dogs started a large gang of old turkey goblers, and I killed two of them, of the biggest sort. I shouldered them up, and moved on, until I got through the harricane, when I was so tired that I laid my goblers down to rest, as they were confounded heavy, and I was mighty tired. While I was resting, my old hound went to a log, and smelt it awhile, and then raised his eyes toward the sky, and cried out. Away he went, and my other dogs with him, and I shouldered up my turkeys again, and followed on as hard as I could drive. They were soon out of sight, and in a very little time I heard them begin to bark. When I got to them, they were barking up a tree, but there was no game there. I concluded it had been a turkey, and that it had flew away.

When they saw me coming, away they went again; and, after a little time, began to bark as before. When I got near them, I found they were barking up the wrong tree again, as there was no game there. They served me in this way three or four times, until I was so infernal mad, that I determined, if I could get near enough, to shoot the old hound at least. With this intention I pushed on the harder, till I came to the edge of an open parara, and looking on before my dogs, I saw in and about the biggest bear that ever was seen in America. He looked, at the distance he was from me, like a large black bull. My dogs were afraid to attack him, and that was the reason they had stop'd so often, that I might overtake them. They were now almost up with him, and I took my goblers from my back and hung them up in a sapling, and broke like a quarter horse after my bear, for the sight of him had put new springs in me. I soon got near to them, but they were just getting into a roaring thicket, and so I couldn't run through it, but had to pick my way along, and had close work even at that.

In a little time I saw the bear climbing up a large black oak-tree, and I crawled on till I got within about eighty yards of him. He was setting with his breast to me; and so I put fresh priming in my gun, and fired at him. At this he raised one of his paws and snorted loudly. I loaded again as quick as I could, and fired as near the same place in his breast as possible. At the crack of my gun here he came tumbling down; and the moment he touched the ground, I heard one of my best dogs cry out. I took my tomahawk in one hand, and my big butcher-knife in the other, and run up within four or five paces of him, at which he let my dog go, and fixed his eyes on me. I got back in all sorts of a hurry, for I know'd if he got hold of me, he would hug me altogether too close for comfort. I went to my gun and hastily loaded her again, and shot him the third time, which killed him good.

I now began to think about getting him home, but I didn't know how far it was. So I left him and started; and in order to find him again, I would blaze a sapling every little distance, which would show me the way back. I continued this till I got within about a mile of home, for there I know'd very well where I was, and that I could easily find the way back to my blazes. When I got home, I took my brother-in-law, and my young man, and four horses, and went back. We got there just before dark, and struck up a fire, and commenced butchering my bear. It was some time in the night before we finished it; and I can assert, on my honour, that I believe he would have weighed six hundred pounds. It was the second largest I ever saw. I killed one, a few years after, that weighed six hundred and seventeen pounds. I now felt fully compensated for my sufferings in going after my powder; and well satisfied that a dog might sometimes be doing a good business, even when he seemed to be barking up the wrong tree. We got our meat home, and I had the pleasure to know that we now had plenty, and that of the best; and I continued through the winter to supply my family abundantly with bear-meat and venison from the woods.

CHAPTER XIII.

I had on hand a great many skins, and so, in the month of February, I packed a horse with them, and taking my eldest son along with me, cut out for a little town called Jackson, situated about forty miles off. We got there well enough, and I sold my skins, and bought me some coffee, and sugar, powder, lead, and salt. I packed them all up in readiness for a start, which I intended to make early the next morning. Morning came, but I concluded, before I started,

194

I would go and take a horn with some of my old fellow-soldiers that I had met with at Jackson.

I did so; and while we were engaged in this, I met with three candidates for the Legislature; a Doctor Butler, who was, by marriage, a nephew to General Jackson, a Major Lynn, and a Mr. McEver, all first-rate men. We all took a horn together, and some person present said to me, "Crockett, you must offer for the Legislature." I told him I lived at least forty miles from any white settlement, and had no thought of becoming a candidate at that time. So we all parted, and I and my little boy went on home.

It was about a week or two after this, that a man came to my house, and told me I was a candidate. I told him not so. But he took out a newspaper from his pocket, and show'd me where I was announced. I said to my wife that this was all a burlesque on me, but I was determined to make it cost the man who had put it there at least the value of the printing, and of the fun he wanted at my expense. So I hired a young man to work in my place on my farm, and turned out myself electioneering. I hadn't been out long, before I found the people began to talk very much about the bear hunter, the man from the cane; and the three gentlemen, who I have already named, soon found it necessary to enter into an agreement to have a sort of caucus at their March court, to determine which of them was the strongest, and the other two was to withdraw and support him. As the court came on, each one of them spread himself, to secure the nomination; but it fell on Dr. Butler, and the rest backed out. The doctor was a clever fellow, and I have often said he was the most talented man I ever run against for any office. His being related to Gen'l. Jackson also helped him on very much; but I was in for it, and I was determined to push ahead and go through, or stick. Their meeting was held in Madison county, which was the strongest in the representative district, which was composed of eleven counties, and they seemed bent on having the member from there.

At this time Col. Alexander was a candidate for Congress, and attending one of his public meetings one day, I walked to where he was treating the people, and he gave me an introduction to several of his acquaintances, and informed them that I was out electioneering. In a little time my competitor, Doctor Butler, came along; he passed by without noticing me, and I suppose, indeed, he did not recognise me. But I hailed him, as I was for all sorts of fun; and when he turned to me, I said to him, "Well, doctor, I suppose they have weighed you out to me; but I should like to know why they fixed your election for March instead of August? This is," said I, "a branfire new way of doing business, if a caucus is to make a representative for the people!" He now discovered who I was, and cried out, "D—n it, Crockett, is that you?"—"Be sure it is," said I, "but I don't want it understood that I have come electioneering. I have just crept out of the cane, to see what discoveries I could make among the white folks." I told him that when I set out electioneering, I would go prepared to put every man on as good footing when I left him as I found him on. I would therefore have me a large buckskin hunting-shirt made, with a couple of pockets holding about a peck each; and that in one I would carry a great big twist of tobacco, and in the other my bottle of liquor; for I knowed when I met a man and offered him a dram, he would throw out his quid of tobacco to take one, and after he had taken his horn, I would out with my twist and give him another chaw. And in this way he would not be worse off than when I found him; and I would be sure to leave him in a first-rate good humour. He said I could beat him electioneering all hollow. I told him I would give him better evidence of that before August, notwithstanding he had many advantages over me, and particularly in the way of money; but I told him that I would go on the products of the country; that I had industrious children, and the best of coon dogs, and they would hunt every night till midnight to support my election; and when the coon fur wa'n't good, I would myself go a wolfing, and shoot down a wolf, and skin his head, and his scalp would be good to me for three dollars, in our state treasury money; and in this way I would get along on the big string. He stood like he was both amused and astonished, and the whole crowd was in a roar of laughter. From this place I returned home, leaving the people in a first-rate way; and I was sure I would do a good business among them. At any rate, I was determined to stand up to my lick-log, salt or no salt.

In a short time there came out two other candidates, a Mr. Shaw and a Mr. Brown. We all ran the race through; and when the election was over, it turned out that I beat them all by a majority of two hundred and forty-seven votes, and was again returned as a member of the Legislature from a new region of the country, without losing a session. This reminded me of the old saying—"A fool for luck, and a poor man for children."

I now served two years in that body from my new district, which was the years 1823 and '24. At the session of 1823, I had a small trial of my independence, and whether I would forsake principle for party, or for the purpose of following after big men.

The term of Col. John Williams had expired, who was a senator in Congress from the state of Tennessee. He was a candidate for another election, and was opposed by Pleasant M. Miller, Esq., who, it was believed, would not be able to beat the colonel. Some two or three others were spoken of, but it was at last concluded that the only man who could beat him was the present "government," General Jackson. So, a few days before the election was to come on, he was sent for to come and run for the senate. He was then in nomination for the presidency; but sure enough he came, and did run as the opponent of Colonel Williams, and beat him too, but not by my vote. The vote was, for Jackson, thirty-five; for Williams, twenty-five. I thought the colonel had honestly discharged his duty, and even the mighty name of Jackson couldn't make me vote against him.

But voting against the old chief was found a mighty up-hill business to all of them except myself. I never would, nor never did, acknowledge I had voted wrong; and I am more certain now that I was right than ever.

I told the people it was the best vote I ever gave; that I had supported the public interest, and cleared my conscience in giving it, instead of gratifying the private ambition of a man.

I let the people know as early as then, that I wouldn't take a collar around my neck with the letters engraved on it,

MY DOG
Andrew Jackson

During these two sessions of the Legislature, nothing else turned up which I think it worth while to mention; and, indeed, I am fearful that I am too particular about many small matters; but if so, my apology is, that I want the world to understand my true history, and how I worked along to rise from a cane-brake to my present station in life.

Col. Alexander was the representative in Congress of the district I lived in, and his vote on the tariff law of 1824 gave a mighty heap of dissatisfaction to his people. They therefore began to talk pretty strong of running me for Congress against him. At last I was called on by a good many to be a candidate. I told the people that I couldn't stand that; it was a step above my knowledge, and I know'd nothing about Congress matters.

However, I was obliged to agree to run, and myself and two other gentlemen came out. But Providence was a little against two of us this hunt, for it was the year that cotton brought twenty-five dollars a hundred; and so Colonel Alexander would get up and tell the people, it was all the good effect of this tariff law; that it had raised the price of their cotton, and that it would raise the price of every thing else they made to sell. I might as well have sung salms over a dead horse, as to try to make the people believe otherwise; for they knowed their cotton had raised, sure enough, and if the colonel hadn't done it, they didn't know what had. So he rather made a mash of me this time, as he beat me exactly two votes, as they counted the polls, though I have always believed that many other things had been as fairly done as that same count.

He went on, and served out his term, and at the end of it cotton was down to six or eight dollars a hundred again; and I concluded I would try him once more, and see how it would go with cotton at the common price, and so I became a candidate.

CHAPTER XIV.

But the reader, I expect, would have no objection to know a little about my employment during the two years while my competitor was in Congress. In this space I had some pretty tuff times, and will relate some few things that happened to me. So here goes, as the boy said when he run by himself.

In the fall of 1825, I concluded I would build two large boats, and load them with pipe staves for market. So I went down to the lake, which was about twenty-five miles from where I lived, and hired some hands to assist me, and went to work; some at boat building, and others to getting staves. I worked on with my hands till the bears got fat, and then I turned out to hunting, to lay in a supply of meat. I soon killed and salted down as many as were necessary for my family; but about this time one of my old neighbours, who had settled down on the lake about twenty-five miles from me, came to my house and told me he wanted me to go down and kill some bears about in his parts. He said they were extremely fat, and very plenty. I know'd that when they were fat, they were easily taken, for a fat bear can't run fast or long. But I asked a bear no favours, no way, further than civility, for I now had eight large dogs, and as fierce as painters; so that a bear stood no chance at all to get away from them. So I went home with him, and then went on down towards the Mississippi, and commenced hunting.

We were out two weeks, and in that time killed fifteen bears. Having now supplied my friend with plenty of meat, I engaged occasionally again with my hands in our boat building, and getting staves. But I at length couldn't stand it any longer without another hunt. So I concluded to take my little son, and cross over the lake, and take a hunt there. We got over, and that evening turned out and killed three bears, in little or no time. The next morning we drove up four forks, and made a sort of scaffold, on which we salted up our meat, so as to have it out of the reach of the wolves, for as soon as we would leave our camp, they would take possession. We had just eat our breakfast, when a company of hunters came to our camp, who had fourteen dogs, but all so poor, that when they would bark they would almost have to lean up against a tree and take a rest. I told them their dogs couldn't run in smell of a bear, and they had better stay at my camp, and feed them on the bones I had cut out of my meat. I left them there, and cut out; but I hadn't gone far, when my dogs took a first-rate start after a very large fat old he-bear, which run right plump towards my camp. I pursued on, but my other hunters had heard my dogs coming, and met them, and killed the bear before I got up with him. I gave him to them, and cut out again for a creek called Big Clover, which wa'n't very far off. Just as I got there, and was entering a cane brake, my dogs all broke and went ahead, and, in a little time, they raised a fuss in the cane, and seemed to be going every way. I listened a while, and found my dogs was in two companies, and that both was in a snorting fight. I sent my little son to one, and I broke for t'other. I got to mine first, and found my dogs had a two-year-old bear down, a-wooling away on him; so I just took out my big butcher, and went up and slap'd it into him, and killed him without shooting. There was five of the dogs in my company. In a short time, I heard my little son fire at his bear; when I went to him he had killed it too. He had two dogs in his team. Just at this moment we heard my other dog barking a short distance off, and all the rest immediately broke to him. We pushed on too, and when we got there, we found he had still a larger bear than either of them we had killed, treed by himself. We killed that one also, which made three we had killed in less than half an hour. We turned in and butchered them, and then started to hunt for water, and a good place to camp. But we had no sooner started, than our dogs took a start after another one, and away they went like a thunder-gust, and was out of hearing in a minute. We followed the way they had gone for some time, but at length we gave up the hope of finding them, and turned back. As we were going back, I came to where a poor fellow was grubbing, and he looked like the very picture of hard times. I asked him what he was doing away there in the woods by himself? He said he was grubbing for a man who intended to settle there; and the reason why he did it was, that he had no meat for his family, and he was working for a little.

I was mighty sorry for the poor fellow, for it was not only a hard, but a very slow way to get meat for a hungry family; so I told him if he would go with me, I would give him more meat than he could get by grubbing in a month. I intended to supply him with meat, and also to get him to assist my little boy in packing in and salting up my bears. He had never seen a bear killed in his life. I told him I had six killed then, and my dogs were hard after another. He went off to his little cabin, which was a short distance in the brush, and his wife was very anxious he should go with me. So we started and went to where I had left my three bears, and made a camp. We then gathered my meat and salted, and scaffled it, as I had done the other. Night now came on, but no word from my dogs yet. I afterwards found they had treed the bear about five miles off, near to a man's house, and had barked at it the whole enduring night. Poor fellows! many a time they looked for me, and wondered why I didn't come, for they knowed there was no mistake in me, and I know'd they were as good as ever fluttered. In the morning, as soon as it was light enough to see, the man took his gun and went to them, and shot the bear, and killed it. My dogs, however, wouldn't have any thing to say to this stranger; so they left him, and came early in the morning back to me. We got our breakfast, and cut out again; and we killed four large and very fat bears that day. We hunted out the week, and in that time we killed seventeen, all of them first-rate. When we closed our hunt, I gave the man over a thousand weight of fine fat bear-meat, which pleased him mightily, and made him feel as rich as a Jew. I saw him the next fall, and he told me he had plenty of meat to do him the whole year from his week's hunt. My son and me now went home. This was the week between Christmas and New-year that we made this hunt.

When I got home, one of my neighbours was out of meat, and wanted me to go back, and let him go with me, to take another hunt. I couldn't refuse; but I told him I was afraid the bear had taken to house by that time, for after they get very fat in the fall and early part of the winter, they go into their holes, in large hollow trees, or into hollow logs, or their cane-houses, or the harricanes; and lie there till spring, like frozen snakes. And one thing about this will seem mighty strange to many people. From about the first of January to about the last of April, these varments lie in their holes altogether. In all that time they have no food to eat; and yet when they come out, they are not an ounce lighter than when they went to house. I don't know the cause of this, and still I know it is a fact; and I leave it for others who have more learning than myself to account for it. They have not a particle of food with them, but they just lie and suck the bottom of their paw all the time. I have killed many of them in their trees, which enables me to speak positively on this subject. However, my neighbour,

whose name was McDaniel, and my little son and me, went on
down to the lake to my second camp, where I had killed my seventeen bears the week before, and turned out to hunting. But we
hunted hard all day without getting a single start. We had carried
but little provisions with us, and the next morning was entirely
out of meat. I sent my son about three miles off, to the house of
an old friend, to get some. The old gentleman was much pleased
to hear I was hunting in those parts, for the year before the bears
had killed a great many of his hogs. He was that day killing his
bacon hogs, and so he gave my son some meat, and sent word to
me that I must come in to his house that evening, that he would
have plenty of feed for my dogs, and some accommodations for
ourselves; but before my son got back, we had gone out hunting,
and in a large cane brake my dogs found a big bear in a cane-
house, which he had fixed for his winter-quarters, as they sometimes do.

When my lead dog found him, and raised the yell, all the rest
broke to him, but none of them entered his house until we got
up. I encouraged my dogs, and they knowed me so well, that I
could have made them seize the old serpent himself, with all his
horns and heads, and cloven foot and ugliness into the bargain,
if he would only have come to light, so that they could have seen
him. They bulged in, and in an instant the bear followed them
out, and I told my friend to shoot him, as he was mighty wrathy
to kill a bear. He did so, and killed him prime. We carried him to
our camp, by which time my son had returned; and after we got
our dinners we packed up, and cut for the house of my old friend,
whose name was Davidson.

We got there, and staid with him that night; and the next morning, having salted up our meat, we left it with him, and started
to take a hunt between the Obion lake and the Red-foot lake; as
there had been a dreadful harricane, which passed between them,
and I was sure there must be a heap of bears in the fallen timber.
We had gone about five miles without seeing any sign at all; but
at length we got on some high cany ridges, and, as we rode along,
I saw a hole in a large black oak, and on examining more closely,
I discovered that a bear had clomb the tree. I could see his tracks
going up, but none coming down, and so I was sure he was in

there. A person who is acquainted with bear-hunting, can tell easy enough when the varment is in the hollow; for as they go up they don't slip a bit, but as they come down they make long scratches with their nails.

My friend was a little ahead of me, but I called him back, and told him there was a bear in that tree, and I must have him out. So we lit from our horses, and I found a small tree which I thought I could fall so as to lodge against my bear tree, and we fell to work chopping it with our tomahawks. I intended, when we lodged the tree against the other, to let my little son go up, and look into the hole, for he could climb like a squirrel. We had chop'd on a little time and stop'd to rest, when I heard my dogs barking mighty severe at some distance from us, and I told my friend I knowed they had a bear; for it is the nature of a dog, when he finds you are hunting bears, to hunt for nothing else; he becomes fond of the meat, and considers other game as "not worth a notice," as old Johnson said of the devil.

We concluded to leave our tree a bit, and went to my dogs, and when we got there, sure enough they had an eternal great big fat bear up a tree, just ready for shooting. My friend again petitioned me for liberty to shoot this one also. I had a little rather not, as the bear was so big, but I couldn't refuse; and so he blazed away, and down came the old fellow like some great log had fell. I now missed one of my dogs, the same that I before spoke of as having treed the bear by himself sometime before, when I had started the three in the cane break. I told my friend that my missing dog had a bear somewhere, just as sure as fate; so I left them to butcher the one we had just killed, and I went up on a piece of high ground to listen for my dog. I heard him barking with all his might some distance off, and I pushed ahead for him. My other dogs hearing him broke to him, and when I got there, sure enough again he had another bear ready treed; if he hadn't, I wish I may be shot. I fired on him, and brought him down; and then went back, and help'd finish butchering the one at which I had left my friend. We then packed both to our tree where we had left my boy. By this time, the little fellow had cut the tree down that we intended to lodge, but it fell the wrong way; he had then feather'd in on the big tree, to cut that, and had found that it was nothing but a shell on the outside, and all doted in the middle, as too many of our big men are in these days, having only an outside appearance. My friend and my son cut away on it, and I went off about a hundred yards with my dogs to keep them from running under the tree when it should fall. On looking back at the hole, I saw the bear's head out of it, looking down at them as they were cutting. I hollered to them to look up, and they did so; and McDaniel catched up his gun, but by this time the bear was out, and coming down the tree. He fired at it, and as soon as it touch'd ground the dogs were all round it, and they had a roll-and-tumble fight to the foot of the hill, where they stop'd him. I ran up, and putting my gun against the bear, fired and killed him. We now had three, and so we made our scaffold and salted them up.

CHAPTER XV.

In the morning I left my son at the camp, and we started on towards the harricane; and when we had went about a mile, we started a very large bear, but we got along mighty slow on account of the cracks in the earth occasioned by the earthquakes. We, however, made out to keep in hearing of the dogs for about three miles, and then we come to the harricane. Here we had to quit our horses, as old Nick himself couldn't have got through it without sneaking it along in the form that he put on, to make a fool of our old grandmother Eve. By this time several of my dogs had got tired and come back; but we went ahead on foot for some little time in the harricane, when we met a bear coming straight to us, and not more than twenty or thirty yards off. I started my tired dogs after him, and McDaniel pursued them, and I went on to where my other dogs were. I had seen the track of the bear they were after, and I knowed he was a screamer. I followed on to about the middle of the harricane; but my dogs pursued him so close, that they made him climb an old stump about twenty feet high. I got in shooting distance of him and fired, but I was all over in such a flutter from fatigue and running, that I couldn't hold steady; but, however, I broke his shoulder, and he fell. I run up and loaded my gun as quick as possible, and shot him again and killed him. When I went to take out my knife to butcher him,

I found I had lost it in coming through the harricane. The vines and briers was so thick that I would sometimes have to get down and crawl like a varment to get through at all; and a vine had, as I supposed, caught in the handle and pulled it out. While I was standing and studying what to do, my friend came to me. He had followed my trail through the harricane, and had found my knife, which was mighty good news to me; as a hunter hates the worst in the world to lose a good dog, or any part of his hunting-tools. I now left McDaniel to butcher the bear, and I went after our horses, and brought them as near as the nature of case would allow. I then took our bags, and went back to where he was; and when we had skin'd the bear, we fleeced off the fat and carried it to our horses at several loads. We then packed it up on our horses, and had a heavy pack of it on each one. We now started and went on till about sunset, when I concluded we must be near our camp; so I hollered and my son answered me, and we moved on in the direction to the camp. We had gone but a little way when I heard my dogs make a warm start again; and I jumped down from my horse and gave him up to my friend, and told him I would follow them. He went on to the camp, and I went ahead after my dogs with all my might for a considerable distance, till at last night came on. The woods were very rough and hilly, and all covered over with cane.

I now was compel'd to move on more slowly; and was frequently falling over logs, and into the cracks made by the earthquakes, so that I was very much afraid I would break my gun. However I went on about three miles, when I came to a good big creek, which I waded. It was very cold, and the creek was about knee-deep; but I felt no great inconvenience from it just then, as I was all over wet with sweat from running, and I felt hot enough. After I got over this creek and out of the cane, which was very thick on all our creeks, I listened for my dogs. I found they had either treed or brought the bear to a stop, as they continued barking in the same place. I pushed on as near in the direction to the noise as I could, till I found the hill was too steep for me to climb, and so I backed and went down the creek some distance till I came to a hollow, and then took up that, till I come to a place where I could climb up the hill. It was mighty dark, and was difficult to see my way or any thing else. When I got up the hill, I found I had passed the dogs; and so I turned and went to them. I found, when I got there, they had treed the bear in a large forked poplar, and it was setting in the fork.

I could see the lump, but not plain enough to shoot with any certainty, as there was no moonlight; and so I set in to hunting for some dry brush to make me a light; but I could find none, though I could find that the ground was torn mightily to pieces by the cracks.

At last I thought I could shoot by guess, and kill him; so I pointed as near the lump as I could, and fired away. But the bear didn't come he only clomb up higher, and got out on a limb, which helped me to see him better. I now loaded up again and fired, but this time he didn't move at all. I commenced loading for a third fire, but the first thing I knowed, the bear was down among my dogs, and they were fighting all around me. I had my big butcher in my belt, and I had a pair of dressed buckskin breeches on. So I took out my knife, and stood, determined, if he should get hold of me, to defend myself in the best way I could. I stood there for some time, and could now and then see a white dog I had, but the rest of them, and the bear, which were dark coloured, I couldn't see at all, it was so miserable dark. They still fought around me, and sometimes within three feet of me; but, at last, the bear got down into one of the cracks, that the earthquakes had made in the ground, about four feet deep, and I could tell the biting end of him by the hollering of my dogs. So I took my gun and pushed the muzzle of it about, till I thought I had it against the main part of his body, and fired; but it happened to be only the fleshy part of his foreleg. With this, he jumped out of the crack, and he and the dogs had another hard fight around me, as before. At last, however, they forced him back into the crack again, as he was when I had shot.

I had laid down my gun in the dark, and I now began to hunt for it; and, while hunting, I got hold of a pole, and I concluded I would punch him awhile with that. I did so, and when I would punch him, the dogs would jump in on him, when he would bite them badly, and they would jump out again. I concluded, as he would take punching so patiently, it might be that he would lie still enough for me to get down in the crack, and feel slowly along till I could find the right place to give him a dig with my butcher. So I got down, and my dogs got in before him and kept his head towards them, till I got along easily up to him; and placing my hand on his rump, felt for his shoulder, just behind which I intended to stick him. I made a lounge with my long knife, and fortunately stuck him right through the heart; at which he just sank down, and I crawled out in a hurry. In a little time my dogs all come out too, and seemed satisfied, which was the way they always had of telling me that they had finished him.

I suffered very much that night with cold, as my leather breeches, and every thing else I had on, was wet and frozen. But I managed to get my bear out of this crack after several hard trials, and so I butchered him, and laid down to try to sleep. But my fire was very bad, and I couldn't find any thing that would burn well to make it any better; and I concluded I should freeze, if I didn't warm myself in some way by exercise. So I got up, and hollered a while, and then I would just jump up and down with all my might, and throw myself into all sorts of motions. But all this wouldn't do; for my blood was now getting cold, and the chills coming all over me. I was so tired, too, that I could hardly walk; but I thought I would do the best I could to save my life, and then, if I died, nobody would be to blame. So I went to a tree about two feet through, and not a limb on it for thirty feet, and I would climb up it to the limbs, and then lock my arms together around it, and slide down to the bottom again. This would make the insides of my legs and arms feel mighty warm and good. I continued this till daylight in the morning, and how often I clomb up my tree and slid down I don't know, but I reckon at least a hundred times.

In the morning I got my bear hung up so as to be safe, and then set out to hunt for my camp. I found it after a while, and McDaniel and my son were very much rejoiced to see me get back, for they were about to give me up for lost. We got our breakfasts, and then secured our meat by building a high scaffold, and covering it over. We had no fear of its spoiling, for the weather was so cold that it couldn't.

We now started after my other bear, which had caused me so

much trouble and suffering; and before we got him, we got a start after another, and took him also. We went on to the creek I had crossed the night before and camped, and then went to where my bear was, that I had killed in the crack. When we examined the place, McDaniel said he wouldn't have gone into it, as I did, for all the bears in the woods.

We took the meat down to our camp and salted it, and also the last one we had killed; intending, in the morning, to make a hunt in the harricane again.

We prepared for resting that night, and I can assure the reader I was in need of it. We had laid down by our fire, and about ten o'clock there came a most terrible earthquake, which shook the earth so, that we were rocked about like we had been in a cradle. We were very much alarmed; for though we were accustomed to feel earthquakes, we were now right in the region which had been torn to pieces by them in 1812, and we thought it might take a notion and swallow us up, like the big fish did Jonah.

In the morning we packed up and moved to the harricane, where we made another camp, and turned out that evening and killed a very large bear, which made eight we had now killed in this hunt. The next morning we entered the harricane again, and in little or no time my dogs were in full cry. We pursued them, and soon came to a thick cane-brake, in which they had stop'd their bear. We got up close to him, as the cane was so thick that we couldn't see more than a few feet. Here I made my friend hold the cane a little open with his gun till I shot the bear, which was a mighty large one. I killed him dead in his tracks. We got him out and butchered him, and in a little time started another and killed him, which now made ten we had killed; and we know'd we couldn't pack any more home, as we had only five horses along; therefore we returned to the camp and salted up all our meat, to be ready for a start homeward next morning.

The morning came, and we packed our horses with the meat, and had as much as they could possibly carry, and sure enough cut out for home. It was about thirty miles, and we reached home the second day. I had now accommodated my neighbour with meat enough to do him, and had killed in all, up to that time, fifty-eight bears, during the fall and winter.

As soon as the time come for them to quit their houses and come out again in the spring, I took a notion to hunt a little more, and in about one month I killed forty-seven more, which made one hundred and five bears I had killed in less than one year from that time.

CHAPTER XVI.

Having now closed my hunting for that winter, I returned to my hands, who were engaged about my boats and staves, and made ready for a trip down the river. I had two boats and about thirty thousand staves, and so I loaded with them, and set out for New Orleans. I got out of the Obion river, in which I had loaded my boats, very well; but when I got into the Mississippi, I found all my hands were bad scared, and in fact I believe I was scared a little the worst of any; for I had never been down the river, and I soon discovered that my pilot was as ignorant of the business as myself. I hadn't gone far before I determined to lash the two boats together; we did so, but it made them so heavy and obstinate, that it was next akin to impossible to do any thing at all with them, or to guide them right in the river.

That evening we fell in company with some Ohio boats; and about night we tried to land, but we could not. The Ohio men hollered to us to kjgo on and run all night. We took their advice, though we had a good deal rather not; but we couldn't do any other way. In a short distance we got into what is called the "Devil's Elbow;" and if any place in the wide creation has its own proper name, I thought it was this. Here we had about the hardest work that I ever was engaged in, in my life, to keep out of danger; and even then we were in it all the while. We twice attempted to land at Wood-yards, which we could see, but couldn't reach.

The people would run out with lights, and try to instruct us how to get to shore; but all in vain. Our boats were so heavy that we couldn't take them much any way, except the way they wanted to go, and just the way the current would carry them. At last we quit trying to land, and concluded just to go ahead as well as we could, for we found we couldn't do any better. Some time in the night I was down in the cabin of one of the boats, sitting by the fire, thinking on what a hobble we had got into; and how much better bear-hunting was on hard land, than floating along on the water, when a fellow had to go ahead whether he was exactly willing or not.

The hatchway into the cabin came slap down, right through the top of the boat; and it was the only way out except a small hole in the side, which we had used for putting our arms through to dip up water before we lashed the boats together.

We were now floating sideways, and the boat I was in was the hindmost as we went. All at once I heard the hands begin to run over the top of the boat in great confusion, and pull with all their might; and the first thing I know'd after this we went broadside full tilt against the head of an island where a large raft of drift timber had lodged. The nature of such a place would be, as every body knows, to suck the boats down, and turn them right under this raft; and the uppermost boat would, of course, be suck'd down and go under first. As soon as we struck, I bulged for my hatchway, as the boat was turning under sure enough. But when I got to it, the water was pouring thro' in a current as large as the hole would let it, and as strong as the weight of the river could force it. I found I couldn't get out here, for the boat was now turned down in such a way, that it was steeper than a house-top. I now thought of the hole in the side, and made my way in a hurry for that. With difficulty I got to it, and when I got there, I found it was too small for me to get out by my own dower, and I began to think that I was in a worse box than ever. But I put my arms through and hollered as loud as I could roar, as the boat I was in hadn't yet quite filled with water up to my head, and the hands who were next to the raft, seeing my arms out, and hearing me holler, seized them, and began to pull. I told them I was sinking, and to pull my arms off, or force me through, for now I know'd well enough it was neck or nothing, come out or sink.

By a violent effort they jerked me through; but I was in a pretty pickle when I got through. I had been sitting without any clothing over my shirt: this was torn off, and I was literally skin'd like a rabbit. I was, however, well pleased to get out in any way, even without shirt or hide; as before I could straighten myself on the boat next to the raft, the one they pull'd me out of went entirely under, and I have never seen it any more to this day. We all escaped on to the raft, where we were compelled to sit all night, about a mile from land on either side. Four of my company were bareheaded, and three bare-footed; and of that number I was one. I reckon I looked like a pretty cracklin ever to get to Congress!!! We had now lost all our loading; and every particle of our clothing, except what little we had on; but over all this, while I was setting there, in the night, floating about on the drift, I felt happier and better off than I ever had in my life before, for I had just made such a marvellous escape, that I had forgot almost every thing else in that; and so I felt prime.

In the morning about sunrise, we saw a boat coming down, and we hailed her. They sent a large skiff, and took us all on board, and carried us down as far as Memphis. Here I met with a friend, that I never can forget as long as I am able to go ahead at any thing; it was a Major Winchester, a merchant of that place: he let us all have hats, and shoes, and some little money to go upon, and so we all parted.

A young man and myself concluded to go on down to Natchez, to see if we could hear any thing of our boats; for we supposed they would float out from the raft, and keep on down the river. We got on a boat at Memphis, that was going down, and so cut out. Our largest boat, we were informed, had been seen about fifty miles below where we stove, and an attempt had been made to land her, but without success, as she was as hard-headed as ever. This was the last of my boats, and of my boating; for it went so badly with me, along at the first, that I hadn't much mind to try it any more. I now returned home again, and as the next August was the Congressional election, I began to turn my attention a little to that matter, as it was beginning to be talked of a good deal among the people.

CHAPTER XVII.
I have, heretofore, informed the reader that I had determined to run this race to see what effect the price of cotton could have again on it. I now had Col. Alexander to run against once more, and also General William Arnold.

I had difficulties enough to fight against this time, as every one will suppose; for I had no money, and a very bad prospect, so far as I know'd, of getting any to help me along. I had, however, a good friend, who sent for me to come and see him. I went, and he was good enough to offer me some money to help me out. I borrowed as much as I thought I needed at the start, and went ahead. My friend also had a good deal of business about over the district at the different courts; and if he now and then slip'd in a good word for me, it is nobody's business. We frequently met at different places, and, as he thought I needed, he would occasionally hand me a little more cash; so I was able to but a little of "the creature," to put my friends in a good humour, as well as the other gentlemen, for they all treat in that country; not to get elected, of course—for that would be against the law; but just, as I before said, to make themselves and their friends feel their keeping a little.

Nobody ever did know how I got money to get along on, till after the election was over, and I had beat my competitors twenty-seven hundred and forty-eight votes. Even the price of cotton couldn't save my friend Aleck this time. My rich friend, who had been so good to me in the way of money, now sent for me, and loaned me a hundred dollars, and told me to go ahead; that that amount would bear my expenses to Congress, and I must then shift for myself. I came on to Washington, and draw'd two hundred and fifty dollars, and purchased with it a check on the bank at Nashville, and enclosed it to my friend; and I may say, in truth, I sent this money with a mighty good will, for I reckon nobody in this world loves a friend better than me, or remembers a kindness longer.

I have now given the close of the election, but I have skip'd entirely over the canvass, of which I will say a very few things in this place; as I know very well how to tell the truth, but not much about placing them in book order, so as to please critics. Col. Alexander was a very clever fellow, and principal surveyor at that time; so much for one of the men I had to run against. My other competitor was a major-general in the militia, and an attorney-general at the law, and quite a smart, clever man also; and so it will be seen I had war work as well as law trick, to stand up under. Taking both together, they make a pretty considerable of a load for any one man to carry. But for war claims, I consider myself behind no man except "the government," and mighty little, if any, behind him; but this the people will have to determine hereafter, as I reckon it won't do to quit the work of "reform and retrenchment" yet for a spell.

But my two competitors seemed some little afraid of the influence of each other, but not to think me in their way at all. They, therefore, were generally working against each other, while I was going ahead for myself, and mixing among the people in the best way I could. I was as cunning as a little red fox, and wouldn't risk my tail in a "committal" trap.

I found the sign was good, almost everywhere I went. On one occasion, while we were in the eastern counties of the district, it happened that we all had to make a speech, and it fell on me to make the first one. I did so after my manner, and it turned pretty much on the old saying, "A short horse is soon curried," as I spoke not very long. Colonel Alexander followed me, and then General Arnold come on.

The general took much pains to reply to Alexander, but didn't so much as let on that there was any such candidate as myself at all. He had been speaking for a considerable time, when a large flock of guinea-fowls came very near to where he was, and set up the most unmerciful chattering that ever was heard, for they are a noisy little brute any way. They so confused the general, that he made a stop, and requested that they might be driven away. I let him finish his speech, and then walking up to him, said aloud, "Well, colonel, you are the first man I ever saw that understood the language of fowls." I told him that he had not had the politeness to name me in his speech, and that when my little friends, the guinea-fowls, had come up and began to holler "Crockett, Crockett, Crockett," he had been ungenerous enough to stop, and drive them all away. This raised a universal shout among the people for me, and the general seemed mighty bad plagued. But he got more plagued than this at the polls in August, as I have stated before.

This election was in 1827, and I can say, on my conscience, that I was, without disguise, the friend and supporter of General Jackson, upon his principles as he laid them down, and as "I understood them," before his election as president. During my two first sessions in Congress, Mr. Adams was president, and I worked along with what was called the Jackson party pretty well. I was re-elected to Congress, in 1829, by an overwhelming majority; and soon after the commencement of this second term, I saw, or thought I did, that it was expected of me that I was to bow to the name of Andrew Jackson, and follow him in all his motions, and mindings, and turnings, even at the expense of my conscience and judgment. Such a thing was new to me, and a total stranger to my principles. I know'd well enough, though, that if I didn't "hurra" for his name, the hue and cry was to be raised against me, and I was to be sacrificed, if possible. His famous, or rather I should say his in-famous, Indian bill was brought forward, and I opposed it from the purest motives in the world. Several of my colleagues got around me, and told me how well they loved me, and that I was ruining myself. They said this was a favourite measure of the president, and I ought to go for it. I told them I believed it was a wicked, unjust measure, and that I should go against it, let the cost to myself be what it might; that I was willing to go with General Jackson in every thing that I believed was honest and right; but, further than this, I wouldn't go for him, or any other man in the whole creation; that I would sooner be honestly and politically d—nd, than hypocritically immortalized. I had been elected by a majority of three thousand five hundred and eighty-five votes, and I believed they were honest men, and wouldn't want me to vote for any unjust notion, to please Jackson or any one else; at any rate, I was of age, and was determined to trust them. I voted against this Indian bill, and my conscience yet tells me that I gave a good honest vote, and one that I believe will not make me ashamed in the day of judgment. I served out my term, and though many amusing things happened, I am not disposed to swell my narrative by inserting them.

When it closed, and I returned home, I found the storm had raised against me sure enough; and it was echoed from side to side, and from end to end of my district, that I had turned against Jackson. This was considered the unpardonable sin. I was hunted down like a wild varment, and in this hunt every little newspaper in the district, and every little pin-hook lawyer was engaged. Indeed, they were ready to print any and every thing that the ingenuity of man could invent against me. Each editor was furnished with the journals of Congress from head-quarters; and hunted out every vote I had missed in four sessions, whether from sickness or not, no matter, and each one was charged against me at eight dollars. In all I had missed about seventy votes, which they made amount to five hundred and sixty dollars; and they contended I had swindled the government out of this sum, as I had received my pay, as other members do. I was now again a candidate in 1830, while all the attempts were making against me; and every one of these little papers kept up a constant war on me, fighting with every scurrilous report they could catch.

Over all I should have been elected, if it hadn't been, that but a few weeks before the election, the little four-pence-ha'penny limbs of the law fell on a plan to defeat me, which had the desired effect. They agreed to spread out over the district, and make appointments for me to speak, almost everywhere, to clear up the Jackson question. They would give me no notice of these appointments, and the people would meet in great crowds to hear what excuse Crockett had to make for quitting Jackson.

But instead of Crockett's being there, this small-fry of lawyers would be there, with their saddle-bags full of the little newspapers and their journals of Congress; and would get up and speak, and read their scurrilous attacks on me, and would then tell the people that I was afraid to attend; and in this way would turn many against me. All this intrigue was kept a profound secret from me, till it was too late to counteract it; and when the election came, I had a majority in seventeen counties, putting all their votes together, but the eighteenth beat me; and so I was left out of Congress during those two years. The people of my district were induced, by these tricks, to take a stay on me for that time; but they have since found out that they were imposed on, and on re-considering my case, have reversed that decision; which, as the Dutchman said, "is as fair a ding as eber was."

When I last declared myself a candidate, I knew that the district would be divided by the Legislature before the election would come on; and I moreover knew, that from the geographical situation of the country, the county of Madison, which was very strong, and which was the county that had given the majority that had beat me in the former race, should be left off from my district. But when the Legislature met, as I have been informed, and I have no doubt of the fact, Mr. Fitzgerald, my competitor, went up, and informed his friends in that body, that if Madison county was left off, he wouldn't run; for "that Crockett could beat Jackson himself in those parts, in any way they could fix it."

The liberal Legislature you know, of course, gave him that county; and it is too clear to admit of dispute, that it was done to make a mash of me. In order to make my district in this way, they had to form the southern district of a string of counties around three sides of mine, or very nearly so. Had my old district been properly divided, it would have made two nice ones, in convenient nice form. But as it is, they are certainly the most unreasonably laid off of any in the state, or perhaps in the nation, or even in the te-total creation.

However, when the election came on, the people of the district, and of Madison county among the rest, seemed disposed to prove to Mr. Fitzgerald and the Jackson Legislature, that they were not to be transferred like hogs, and horses, and cattle in the market; and they determined that I shouldn't be broke down, though I had to carry Jackson, and the enemies of the bank, and the legislative works all at once. I had Mr. Fitzgerald, it is true, for my open competitor, but he was helped along by all his little lawyers again, headed by old Black Hawk, as he is sometimes called, (alias) Adam Huntsman, with all his talents for writing "Chronicles," and such like foolish stuff.

But one good thing was, and I must record it, the papers in the district were now beginning to say "fair play a little," and they would publish on both sides of the question. The contest was a warm one, and the battle well-fought; but I gained the day, and the Jackson horse was left a little behind. When the polls were compared, it turned out I had beat Fitz just two hundred and two votes, having made a mash of all their intrigues. After all this, the reader will perceive that I am now here in Congress, this 28th day of January, in the year of our Lord one thousand eight hundred and thirty-four; and that, what is more agreeable to my feelings as a freeman, I am at liberty to vote as my conscience and judgment dictates to be right, without the yoke of any party on me, or the driver at my heels, with his whip in hand, commanding me to ge-wo-haw, just at his pleasure. Look at my arms, you will find no party hand-cuff on them! Look at my neck, you will not find there any collar, with the engraving

MY DOG. Andrew Jackson.

But you will find me standing up to my rack, as the people's faithful representative, and the public's most obedient, very humble servant, David Crockett.

The End

Our Source for David Crockett's Autobiography

Project Gutenberg is synonymous with the free distribution of electronic works in formats readable by the widest variety of computers including obsolete, old, middle-aged and new computers. It exists because of the efforts of hundreds of volunteers and donations from people in all walks of life.

Most people start at our Web site which has the main PG search facility:

http://www.gutenberg.org

Parallels between David Crockett and James P. Crockett III

1. Believed a rifle was a powerful thing for a man to possess
2. Loved telling their stories of their time in the wild
3. Large families (Davy - 5th of 9)(James P. - 7th of 12)
4. Members of the Crockett family lineage
5. Both served as soldiers (David - Creek Indian War, Texas Revolution, James P. -World War I)
6. Born outside of Texas; both died in Texas
7. Named rifles "Ol Betsy' and 'Pea-shooter'
8. Won shooting contests in their youth (prize money)
9. Had nicknames: "Davy" and "Jimmy Highpockets"
10. Married twice; two families; both men sired six offspring

David Crockett

Three girls, three boys;
First marriage to Mary 'Polly' Finley in 1806
John Wesley Crockett
William Finley Crockett
Margaret Finley Crockett

Second marriage Elizabeth Patton in 1815:
Robert Patton Crockett
Rebecca Elvira Crockett
Matilda Crockett

James P. Crockett III

Four girls, two boys (twins)
First marriage to Josiah Vickerous Jackson King
Mildred Elaine Crockett Roberson
Wanda

Second marriage to Lillie Mae Reed Crockett in 1927
Julia Mae Crockett
Billie Sue Wade Crockett
James David Crockett (twin)
John Patterson Crockett (twin)

Glossary

Difference between Ancestry and Lineage

The terms "ancestry" and "lineage" are closely related and often used interchangeably, but they have distinct nuances in their meanings and usage:

- Ancestry refers to one's familial background or heritage, encompassing all of one's forebears or ancestors. It's a broad term that includes all the people from whom one is descended, not limited to a direct line but also covering a wider network of relatives, including those not in the direct line of descent.

- Ancestry emphasizes the collective aspect of one's heritage from a wide array of ancestors, including their ethnic, cultural, or national backgrounds. It's often discussed in the context of genealogy, genetic history, and the study of one's family tree, encompassing both direct ancestors and collateral relatives (like cousins, aunts, uncles, etc.).

- People might explore their ancestry for insights into their genetic makeup, health predispositions, cultural heritage, and historical migrations of their families.

- Lineage is more focused on the direct line of descent from an ancestor. It traces the succession of individuals from an ancestor, typically focusing on a particular family line or descent through generations. This can be through the paternal line (patrilineal), maternal line (matrilineal), or both.

- Lineage emphasizes a direct connection between ancestors and descendants, often used in contexts where inheritance, succession, or the transmission of titles, rights, or properties is concerned. It is also relevant in discussions about the continuity of family names, traditions, or occupations.

- In cultural or social contexts, lineage might be significant in societies where pedigree, inheritance, or the tracing of one's roots through a specific line is important for social status, rights, or membership in certain groups.

In summary, ancestry offers a broader look at one's family background, including a wide network of relatives and ethnic heritage, while lineage focuses more narrowly on the direct descent from ancestors, often with implications for inheritance, traditions, and family continuity.

Assets

In the context of family heritage, "assets" can refer to various tangible and intangible elements that are inherited or passed down through generations within a family. These assets are not just financial or material but also encompass cultural, historical, and sentimental values. They contribute to a family's identity, legacy, and continuity over time. Here are some key types of assets in family heritage:

- Material or Financial Assets: These include property, land, buildings, jewelry, heirlooms, and other physical items of value. Financial assets might also comprise investments, savings, or funds that have been accumulated and passed down through generations.

- Cultural Assets: These are the traditions, customs, languages, and crafts that are unique to a family and are often rooted in the wider cultural background from which the family originates. Cultural assets can include family recipes, traditional clothing, art, music, and dance forms.

- Historical Assets: These encompass the family history, stories, and records that detail the lineage, accomplishments, struggles, and significant events of ancestors. They can include family trees, genealogical records, diaries, letters, photographs, and other documents.

- Sentimental Assets: Items or traditions that may not have significant financial value but hold emotional significance for the family. This could include family photographs, keepsakes, medals, or awards won by family members, and even stories or anecdotes passed down orally.

- Intellectual and Educational Assets: The knowledge, skills, educational achievements, and professional networks developed by family members can also be considered assets. These often provide social and economic mobility to subsequent generations.

- Social and Community Assets: The relationships and standing a family has within their community, including friendships, affiliations with community groups, or roles in local history.

In essence, assets in family heritage represent a blend of tangible and intangible elements that are valued not only for their economic worth but also for their role in maintaining and conveying family identity, history, and values across generations.

Family

The concept of "family" is broad and can be defined in various ways, depending on the context and the cultural, social, and personal perspectives. Generally, a family is a group of individuals who are related to each other through blood (biological), legal ties (such as marriage or adoption), or emotional bonds. Here are some key aspects of the definition of a family:

- Biological Connections: In its most traditional sense, a family consists of individuals connected by blood relationships, such as parents and their children, and extends to a wider kinship network including grandparents, aunts, uncles, cousins, etc.

- Legal and Social Bonds: Families also include relationships formed through marriage (spouses, in-laws) and adoption. Legal ties often create family bonds that are as significant as biological connections.

- Nuclear and Extended Family: The nuclear family typically refers to parents and their children living together. An extended family includes a broader network of relatives such as grandparents, aunts, uncles, and cousins, sometimes living together or maintaining close relationships.

- Emotional and Supportive Bonds: A family is often characterized by emotional bonds, support, love, and care among its members. It serves as the primary social unit where individuals learn values, norms, and social skills.

- Household Family: In a more practical sense, a family can refer to all individuals living in the same household, who may or may not be related by blood or marriage.

- Cultural and Societal Variations: The definition of family can vary significantly across different cultures and societies. In some cultures, family structures are more extended and integrated, while in others, the concept of family is more centered on the nuclear unit.

- Changing Dynamics: The concept of family has evolved and continues to change, reflecting broader social, economic, and cultural trends. This includes recognition of single-parent families and cohabiting families.

- Functional Perspective: From a sociological perspective, families are fundamental units of society that fulfill essential functions such as the upbringing and socialization of children, providing emotional and economic support to its members, and ensuring the continuation of societal values and culture.

In summary, family is a dynamic and multifaceted concept that encompasses a range of relationships and structures, shaped by biological, legal, emotional, cultural, and societal factors.

Family Tree

A family tree, also known as a genealogical tree, is a chart or diagram representing family relationships in a conventional tree structure. This visual representation shows the relationships among various family members across different generations in a graphical format. Typically, a family tree starts with the oldest generations at the top and branches downwards to the younger generations.

Key features of a family tree include:
- Ancestors and Descendants: It includes ancestors (like parents,

grandparents, great-grandparents) and descendants (like children, grandchildren).

- Names and Dates: Most family trees will include the names of the family members, and often their birth, marriage, and death dates.
- Connections: Lines or branches connect individuals to show relationships, particularly parent-child and marital relationships.
- Generational Layers: Each generation forms a new layer or level in the tree, making it easy to see the lineage and generational gaps.

Family trees can range from simple diagrams showing just immediate family members to extensive trees tracing lineage back several generations. They can be used for various purposes, including understanding family history, medical histories, and in legal contexts. With advances in technology, digital family trees have become popular, allowing for the integration of photographs, documents, and detailed notes about each individual.

Genealogy

Genealogy is the study of families, family history, and the tracing of their lineages. It involves the systematic research of family ancestries and histories and often includes the creation of a family tree or pedigree chart. Genealogy uses historical records, genetic analysis, and other records to obtain information about a family and to demonstrate kinship and pedigrees of its members. The field combines elements of history, sociology, and anthropology to understand family structures, relationships, and the historical contexts in which they developed. Genealogists often seek to understand not just where and when people lived, but also their lifestyles, biographies, and motivations. This often requires—or leads to—knowledge of antique laws, old political boundaries, migration trends, and historical socioeconomic or religious conditions.

The word 'genealogy' has its origins in the Greek language. It is derived from two Greek words: "genea" (γενεά) meaning "generation" or "descent" and "logos" (λόγος) meaning "knowledge," "study," or "word." Literally translated, genealogy means the study or knowledge of generations or descent.

The term made its way into English through the Late Latin "genealogia," which also means the study or account of family descent. Over time, the term has come to specifically refer to the study of family history and lineage, involving the tracing and documentation of ancestral lines and the connections between members of a family across generations. The practice of genealogy often involves compiling extensive family trees and gathering historical records, such as birth, marriage, and death certificates, to establish familial relationships and heritage. Genealogy can be pursued as a hobby, for legal reasons, or as a profession. It often intersects with historical research and has seen a surge in interest with the advent of online databases and DNA testing services.

"Genealogy" and "Genealogical"

The difference between "genealogy" and "genealogical" primarily lies in their parts of speech and their usage in sentences, reflecting their roles in describing aspects of family history research:

- Genealogy (Noun): This term refers to the study of family ancestries and histories. It involves researching lineages, tracing family pedigrees, and constructing family trees. Genealogy is the discipline or activity of understanding how individuals are related to one another within a family or across families, often involving the collection of historical documents, oral histories, and genetic analysis to trace kinship and lineage.

- Example: "She spent years compiling a comprehensive genealogy of her ancestors, tracing her family back several centuries."

- Genealogical (Adjective): This term is used to describe anything related to the study of genealogy. It modifies nouns and refers to the aspects, methods, or materials pertaining to the research, documentation, and analysis of family histories. Genealogical can describe tools, records, studies, or interests that are part of or useful in the practice of genealogy.

- Example: "He visited the library to access its genealogical records, hoping to find more information about his great-grandparents."

In summary, "genealogy" is the noun that denotes the field of study itself, focusing on family histories and lineage tracing, while "genealogical" is an adjective that describes things related to or pertaining to the study of genealogy.

Heritage

Heritage refers to the range of cultural, historical, and natural assets passed down from previous generations to the present. It encompasses a wide variety of elements, including:

- Cultural Heritage: This includes traditions, languages, knowledge, skills, artworks, buildings, monuments, and literature that are inherited from past generations. Cultural heritage can be tangible, like artifacts, architecture, and landscapes, or intangible, like folklore, traditions, and languages.

- Natural Heritage: This consists of naturally occurring landscapes, ecosystems, and biodiversity that are considered valuable for their aesthetic, ecological, or scientific significance.

- Historical Heritage: This is concerned with significant events, figures, or developments in history. It includes historical sites, documents, and other artifacts that have historical significance.

Heritage is not just about preservation of the past; it also involves the active transmission of these assets, values, and lessons to future generations. The concept of heritage is fundamental to the fields of archaeology, anthropology, history, and conservation. It's often associated with national pride and identity, as well as with the global responsibility to protect and preserve diverse cultures and ecosystems. Heritage is frequently under the guardianship of national and international laws and organizations, such as UNESCO, which work to protect and maintain these valuable assets for future generations.

Lineage

Lineage refers to the direct descent from an ancestor or line of ancestors, typically traced through generations. It is a concept central to genealogy, anthropology, and other social sciences where understanding the succession of generations is crucial. Lineage can be matrilineal (tracing descent through the mother's line), patrilineal (tracing through the father's line), or bilateral (acknowledging both sides equally).

In the context of human societies, lineage plays a significant role in determining inheritance, succession, and social status. It's often used to establish connections to ancestors, sometimes for the purposes of claiming rights, titles, or heritage. Lineage is also important in animal breeding and plant cultivation, where it's used to track genetic qualities and heritage.

The concept of lineage extends beyond biological descent and can include cultural or ideological lineage, where ideas, practices, or professions are passed down through generations, not necessarily within the same family.

Lineal Descent

Lineal descent refers to the direct line of ancestry or descent from an individual to their ancestors or descendants. This concept is a key aspect in genealogy and family history research. Lineal descent follows a straight line from an ancestor to a descendant, typically encompassing relationships like parents to children, grandparents to grandchildren, and so on, moving either upwards (ascending) or downwards (descending) through the generations. Key characteristics of lineal descent include:

- Direct Ancestry: It involves a direct bloodline or biological connection. Adopted children, stepchildren, and in-laws, while part of a family, are not considered part of the lineal descent unless there is a biological connection.

- Generation Tracking: Lineal descent helps in tracking and establishing generational relationships, crucial for understanding family history, lineage, and inheritance patterns.

- Legal and Inheritance Implications: In legal contexts, lineal descent is often important for matters of inheritance, succession, and determining heirs.

- Genealogical Research: For genealogists, establishing lineal descent is crucial in creating accurate family trees and understanding ancestral connections.

- Cultural Significance: In many cultures, lineal descent plays a vital role in defining family relationships, inheritance rights, and social status.

Lineal descent contrasts with collateral descent, which involves relatives who are not directly in one's line of descent, such as siblings, cousins, aunts, and uncles.

Muster

In genealogical terms, a "muster" typically refers to a military muster, which is a gathering, listing, or enrollment of troops for inspection, roll call, or service. Muster records are significant historical documents that genealogists often use to trace ancestors who served in the military. These records can provide various details about military service members, including their names, ranks, units, and dates of service.

Key aspects of a muster in genealogy include:

- Military Service Documentation: Muster rolls were used to document the service of soldiers in a specific military unit at a particular time. They were akin to attendance records, showing who was present or absent at the time of the muster.

- Identification of Ancestors: For genealogists, muster rolls can be valuable in identifying ancestors who served in the military, often providing a starting point for further research into their military service and life.

- Details on Military Units: These records can provide information about the specific military units in which an ancestor served, which can be helpful for understanding their role in historical military engagements or wars.

- Historical Context: Muster records can offer insights into the historical context of an ancestor's military service, including where and when they served, and potentially, details about military campaigns and battles.

- Additional Personal Information: Depending on the record, muster rolls might include additional personal details such as age, physical description, place of birth, or occupation.

Muster records are often found in military archives, national archives, and other historical record repositories. They are a key resource for those conducting genealogical research on ancestors with military backgrounds.

Record

In genealogy, the term "record" refers to any type of documented information that can be used to trace and construct family histories. Records are fundamental tools for genealogists, providing evidence of an individual's life, relationships, and events. Here are some key aspects of records in genealogy:

- Types of Records: There are various types of records used in genealogical research. Common examples include birth, marriage, and death certificates; census records; wills and probate records; land records; military service records; immigration and naturalization records; and church records such as baptisms, marriages, and burials

- Information Contained: Genealogical records typically contain vital information about individuals and families, such as names, dates, places, relationships, occupations, and other relevant data.

- Sources of Records: These records can be found in numerous places, including government archives, church archives, local courthouses, libraries, and online databases.

- Primary vs. Secondary Records: Records are often categorized as primary or secondary sources. Primary sources are documents created at or near the time of an event, like birth certificates or marriage registers. Secondary sources are records that are created well after an event has occurred and might include compiled family histories or books.

- Authenticity and Accuracy: Genealogists assess the authenticity and accuracy of records to ensure reliable research. This involves evaluating the originality of the document, the reliability of the informant, and the consistency of the information with other known facts.

- Citing Records: Proper citation of records is important in genealogical research to maintain the credibility and reproducibility of the research. Citations include information about where the record was found and its specific details.

- Digital Records: With advances in technology, many records have been digitized and are available online, making genealogical research more accessible to a wider audience.

- Privacy and Accessibility: Some records may have restrictions on access due to privacy laws, especially for more recent records. Researchers often need to consider these legal aspects when seeking out records.

Genealogical records are vital for constructing accurate and well-documented family trees and histories. They serve as the building blocks for understanding ancestors' lives and the historical contexts in which they lived.

About the Authors

Mark Standley, PhD
Mark is a researcher and writer. His books are about families curating their possessions in a digital future, learning to become an old man, teaching Jesus, and outdoor skills. He is the grandson of James P. Crockett III (Jimmy Highpockets) and the fourth great grand nephew of David Crockett. Researching this book includes his path to membership of the Sons of the American Revolution (SAR). He is proud parent of two adult children.

Connie Fluegel, MA
Connie has been researching her family genealogy since she was in the third grade. She is a retired educator and a proud mother and grandmother. After obtaining her Masters degree from the University of Minnesota, she moved to Texas where she began her career in adult education at the University of Texas, M.D. Anderson Cancer Center. She is a member of the Daughters of the American Revolution (DAR). Her life-long goal is to love God, build relationships, help others learn and grow.

website: answers.academy

www.ingramcontent.com/pod-product-compliance
Lightning Source LLC
Chambersburg PA
CBHW070802280326
41934CB00012B/3024